Animal Soul Contracts

Sacred Agreements for Shared Evolution

TAMMY BILLUPS

Bear & Company
Rochester, Vermont

Bear & Company
One Park Street
Rochester, Vermont 05767
www.BearandCompanyBooks.com

Text stock is SFI certified

Bear & Company is a division of Inner Traditions International

Cataloging-in-Publication Data for this title is available from the Library of Congress

ISBN 978-1-59143-364-4 (print)
ISBN 978-1-59143-365-1 (ebook)

Printed and bound in the United States by Lake Book Manufacturing, Inc. The text stock is SFI certified. The Sustainable Forestry Initiative® program promotes sustainable forest management.

10 9 8 7 6 5 4 3 2

Text design and layout by Priscilla Baker
This book was typeset in Garamond Premier Pro with Ryo, Gill Sans, Legacy Sans, and SM Gothic used as display typefaces

To send correspondence to the author of this book, mail a first-class letter to the author c/o Inner Traditions • Bear & Company, One Park Street, Rochester, VT 05767, and we will forward the communication, or contact the author directly at **www.tammybillups.com**.

For those who courageously and repeatedly share transformational soul journeys with their beloved animal companions.

My newest teachers, Bodhi and Rumi.
Photo by Lynn Johnson Photography

Contents

∞♡

Not the ones speaking the same language, but sharing the same feeling understand each other.

RUMI

Healing Animals and People Together

J. Zohara Meyerhoff Hieronimus

Have you ever wondered why of all the dogs or cats or other domesticated animals in the world, a certain one, or certain breed or animal attracts you? Have you ever felt that an animal found *you* as much as you found *them?* Or have you noticed how your animal companion knows when you are sad, exhibits happiness when you do, or even manifests illnesses that are like your own? It's said that people and their dogs look alike. But what does this really mean at a deeper level? Tammy Billups's book *Animal Soul Contracts* and the therapeutic work she shares demonstrates that our animal connections go way beyond how we feel about their presence in our lives. Ultimately, she claims, we come to Earth together to experience and share greater love. How we get there is our life's journey.

Billups's therapeutic work, showcased in this book, shows us that the Higher Soul Selves of both animals and humans have often come to Earth planning to share life together. Be they young or old, new or ancient in our lives, we share prearranged contracts. The life-to-life connection between humans seems well substantiated, so why not with our animals too? Humans about to cross over before their body dies will sometimes recognize a deceased loved one, greeting them. Others might say, "I see Skippy," or "I see Little Lady" referring to a deceased childhood pet. There is evidence worldwide that people of the Earth believe animals accompany us on our journey on Earth and in the afterlife as well. Billups documents this reality in her fascinating life journey as a healer of both humans and animals. The animals we share our lives with, as Billups so elegantly demonstrates, are not just our companions, they are our teachers too. As beings of the "now," animals are constantly reflecting us—our emotional, mental, physical, energetic, and soul patterns. Showcasing the numerous true stories of her clients, humans, and animals, Billups reveals a substantial body of testimony as to why Tandem Healing sessions—working with an animal and their human companion(s) simultaneously—can be key to the greatest healings for both.

Why?

If we and the animals around us have a soul contract to "do life together," all the while mirroring each other energetically as Billups explains, then our issues become their issues and theirs become ours. Our lives are so deeply intertwined and the bond substantial. Therefore, as Billups discovered and practices, trans-species companion healing accelerates both human and animal wellness.

This approach to consciousness and healing adds a new dimension to trans-species communication and the therapeutic fields of psychology and health. It's something I am so enthusiastic about, given that I am both a lifelong animal healer and telepath myself. Billups brings a unique set of talents and personal life experiences that led her on this path that resulted in her eventual discovery of the therapeutic value of healing *with* animals, including livestock and wild animals we meet or care for and the ecosystems we are tasked to preserve.

From issues of separation anxiety to overstepping boundaries, our animals are teaching us every day what we look like, how we behave, and what we imagine are the possibilities that await us when we decide to share our lives in reciprocity with our animal kin. As our mirrors, they really want to say to us, as Billups accentuates, that "love is the healer and animals and humans are the beneficiaries." As she notes in her book, animals "listen without judgment, love unconditionally, and serve others in ways we can only hope to duplicate in this life." I agree wholeheartedly.

Billups gives everyone the tools for deeper relations with our animal kin, be they living or deceased, and reveals—in so many true-life stories of animals and their human companions—that love, the Earth blessing for all sentience, is the state of being in relationship with open hearts and minds. *Animal Soul Contracts* offers us a broader therapeutic understanding of how mirroring can become a gift and a vital healing part of the evolutionary journey that animals and humans share together.

J. ZOHARA MEYERHOFF HIERONIMUS has been called a visionary and futurist. She is an award-winning radio broadcaster and author, as well as a social justice, environmental, and animal rights activist. She is a pioneer in holistic health care and founded the Ruscombe Mansion Community Health Center in 1985 in Baltimore, Maryland. She is as well a trans-species telepath who communicates with animals both wild and domestic. Zohara is also well known as a broadcasting personality, having hosted numerous radio shows over the past thirty years. With lifelong participation in the esoteric sciences, global economics, and leading-edge research, Zohara currently cohosts *21st Century Radio,* airing on WCBM 680 Baltimore. Her artwork has been featured in public shows, and her digital photography is archived online in various forums.

Conscious Soul Journeys

The year 2000 is forever embedded in my memory because it arrived with the most valuable gifts I've ever received. As a result of experiencing several unexpected losses, my soul's deepest desires were unlocked and I was forever changed. I embarked on a transformational soul journey and a new path in life. The invaluable gifts of self-discovery, inner healing, and profound love and spiritual connection all landed squarely in my heart that year, along with an overwhelming sense of gratitude.

And as you might imagine, when a person begins an inner healing journey, some days are unpleasant. Emotions that'd been safely suppressed since early childhood were restless and longed to be released. It was as if I'd turned on the faucets to free my pain and was unable to turn them off. Undoubtedly my soul signed up for a quick awakening process so I could embrace a new way of *being* and begin my work with animals and their people.

I'll never forget an experience I had one night during that initiatory year. It'd been an emotionally challenging day, and I had difficulty falling asleep but eventually drifted off. An hour or so later, I began to wake up for some reason. It felt as though

I was coming out of a deep, dark place. I have no recollection of having been dreaming, but I could feel my entire body vibrating and perpetually shaking. Then I became aware of a noise— it sounded like a cat meowing far off in the distance, and I was drawn to it like a magnet. Finally I was able to fully wake up, and the shaking instantly stopped.

Upon opening my eyes, I was astounded to see my cat Vasi standing firmly on my chest with her head directly in front of my face, meowing louder than I thought she was capable of. Her purposeful actions on my behalf were not only surprising, they enlightened me as to just how much our animals are tuned into a higher frequency of service.

Six years prior, I'd adopted three-month-old Vasi to fix a problem in the house. My other two cats, Khalua and Bailey, weren't getting along, and it was affecting Khalua's health. I had a strong sense that a third cat would somehow be able to reinstate harmony in their hearts. Ask any cat behavioral expert if that solution typically works, and they'll probably look at you sideways and begin to chuckle.

Those experts couldn't have known, however, that Vasi and I had deliberately designed a soul contract for her to be the peacemaker. From the moment she arrived in the home, we all felt better. Vasi was independent, secure, and grounded, and unless Khalua or Bailey needed some of her magic, she peacefully kept to herself. Vasi was an old soul on a grace-filled mission.

I'm uncertain exactly what was happening to me on the night she persistently followed her instincts to awaken me, but her extraordinary actions modeled a behavior I continually strive to emulate. With ease and grace, she simply followed her guidance to courageously help and serve as needed.

A few months after that night, she came to me in a dream.

She told me (telepathically) that it was her time to leave. Then I noticed a key on a string dangling from her front right paw. She'd been carrying the key on my behalf, she informed me, but was giving it back to me because I was now "ready."

Vasi passed hours later. It wasn't until I learned about the soul contracts we share with our animals that I fully comprehended how Vasi and I had planned the events of our lives together, even her early departure. We'd scheduled our paths to intersect and intentionally joined forces to clear karma and fulfill several soul contracts.

Vasi's early passing was an emotionally difficult loss for me to recover from, but the awareness of our sacred soul partnership provided much needed consolation. She blessed me with six years of being in the presence of *grace*. Grace is one of the many Pinnacle Teaching virtues that our animals can agree to model and emulate for us to integrate.

 Animals help us to believe in something greater than our human experience.

They model a way of being that we can strive to duplicate in our own lives, and this gives us hope. People willingly give animals their openhearted trust and love. And in turn, animals eagerly sign up to play a significant role in the soul advancement of their person.

Prior to my awakening, I'd seen far too many "coincidences" with my animal companions, which led me to believe that there must be something more transpiring than meets the eye. From early on in my practice and holistic health studies I've been intent on finding the higher purpose held within each animal-human alliance.

Once I began working with both animals and their people, it became abundantly clear that indeed there is a higher purpose and soul mission that travels beyond the unconditional love and companionship animals provide. As a result of working with thousands of two- and four-legged clients, the seven levels of interaction and types of soul agreements came forth into my awareness.

I wholeheartedly wrote this book with the hope that its contents promote a new level of healing, harmony, and peace for you *and* your animals (past and present) to generate more love in all aspects of your lives. *Animal Soul Contracts* will reveal the meaningful reasons you are together, and how your lives can be radically improved through your awareness of the soul agreements.

Woven throughout the book there are many true-life, relatable, genuine stories to boost your understanding of the soul agreements you planned with your beloved animals. I worked closely with each person featured in the book to ensure accuracy and factual integrity in each story and example. Every photo that follows a story is of the actual animal discussed in the story, and sometimes "their person" decided to join them. Several people chose to remain anonymous, however, so *their* names have been changed to protect their identity.

The remarkable people in each story shared one commonality; every person was willing to look within themselves to heal and evolve alongside their animals for their mutual well-being. The inspirational Tandem Healing stories portray what can transpire when you engage in a conscious soul journey with your animal. The people and animals in each story will motivate you to delve deeper into the wisdom of *your* animal soul contracts, so you can simultaneously heal and enhance the quality of your time together. Soul contracts and agreements are not one-sided. They are designed to be mutually beneficial.

Additionally, I've shared several personal stories about my

own animal companions, disclosing what they have so eloquently taught me through experiences that were paramount to our mutual growth. After adopting new cat companions Bodhi and Rumi last year, I discovered our unexpected soul history, which beckoned to be revealed. Bodhi's story was especially difficult to write, and I almost didn't, but I'm conscious of its potential to bring healing to those with similar wounds. Each animal I've shared my heart and home with has been a guiding light that illuminated the path to writing this book.

Animal Soul Contracts will guide you to the heart and soul of your animal partnerships and shed light on how you can more easily navigate this earthly ride together. When you engage in a conscious soul journey with your animal companions, your shared love will expand in unimaginable and beautiful ways, enabling you to enrich the lives of countless others.

Having respect for animals makes us better humans.

JANE GOODALL

1

Animal-Human Soul Talk

Increasingly people are waking up to the realization that there is so much more to their relationship with their animal companions than meets the eye. Minds and hearts are opening to a new level of awareness and embracing the gifts that go hand in hand with having a more conscious animal-human partnership. People are searching for the higher purpose in the heart of their relationships and are more willing to look at what their animal companions are teaching them about themselves.

This is truly extraordinary. Animal lovers are keenly aware of the benefits people receive from the unconditional love and acceptance offered by their beloved companions. An animal's love can lower blood pressure and unleash a plethora of feel-good hormones in humans. They are masters at helping innumerable people feel loved, and they help them to relax into the present moment. In this, animals are great relievers of stress. Yes, animals are master healers. Sharing your life with an animal can be likened to being touched by an angel.

And yet there is abundantly more to each animal's evolutionary journey than just their relationship with human beings. What people might not be aware of is that animals, like humans, are on their own amazing soul journeys of growth, learning, and service. In addition, animal lovers may also be unaware that humans and animals who find their lives intertwined are together by design, not by accident; there is no such thing as coincidence.

This design takes the form of a soul contract. Before either the person or animal in a specific relationship incarnated into their current physical form, their Higher Self, their soul, agreed in advance to enter into a sacred partnership to mutually heal, evolve, and love like never before. The animals that show up in your life have a mission and purpose, just as you do. With divine intentions, animals and their human companions create soul contracts to help each other reach their highest potential.

It is more commonly known that we have soul contracts with other people, but through my work with both animals and the people who love them it has become remarkably clear that there are similar agreements between humans and animals, particularly the ones we share space with. Your hearts are and will forever be linked through your steadfast and loving commitment to mutual transformation.

Your souls are always communicating with each other, and how your "soul talk" shows up in your interactions with animals is fascinating. Fasten your animal-loving seat belt because you are about to embark on a journey that reveals the higher-purpose possibilities held within every animal-human soul collaboration.

THE HEALER

For the record, never have I said I wanted to be a writer. It still feels strange to say I'm an author, but I'm leaning into that more and more. *I'm a healer.* Even when I wasn't yet embracing my soul's purpose, I had a desire and longing to help others suffer less and heal their emotional wounds. Being a healer is wired into my spiritual DNA.

Twenty years ago, after my first animal companion— my cat Khalua—had passed from colon cancer, I was sitting at home releasing an abundance of grief. In that vulnerable moment I implored to the heavens that her spirit come back and live with me. In the month prior, my mother had died, and her final weeks had provided me with undeniable proof that the spirit lives on and is greeted on the other side by those who have passed before them.

In my despair over Khalua's passing, I was concerned there was no one on the other side to greet *her*. My mother was not a cat lover, so I assumed she wasn't an option. As a result, I pleaded to a higher power to let Khalua's spirit return to live with me.

Later that same evening I was astonished and surprised to unexpectedly actually *see* Khalua's spirit going about her normal routine. I was astounded and amazed by this newfound ability I'd seemed to have instantaneously acquired. After that I spent a considerable amount of time trying to hone my skill set, which quickly led to my new (not) normal reality of continuously seeing, sensing, and feeling energy. I aspired to learn more about the other dimensions I suddenly had access to. At this point in my life, I was at the peak of a successful, albeit dissatisfying, career, and I wondered why this experience had come about at that particular time.

Thus began the most incredible and transformational year of my life. I'll be forever grateful for the endless gifts that emerged in that life-changing year. One of the most profound was that I was catapulted onto the path of my soul's deepest longing: the path of the healer.

Since joyfully embracing my life's passion and purpose all

those years ago, it would be fair to say that I now define success much differently than I did back then. I'm also confident that the events and experiences that led up to that year, and since then, were planned by my soul. I've received a lot of help along the way with the soul agreements I have with animals, humans, and the band of light beings that have continuously supported my development.

My best teachers in my practice continue to be every two-, four-, (and sometimes three-) legged client I'm blessed to work with. My intention to lighten the emotional load that people and animals carry is deeply ingrained in every fiber of my being. I'm grateful and eager to share what I have learned and observed through my work to help animals and humans heal and evolve *together*.

When I began my healing practice, working with animals wasn't on the radar. My initial focus was helping people heal through a transformational holistic healing modality that I'd personally experienced miraculous results with. It was curiosity that prompted me to ask friends if I could work on their animal companions.

Being an avid animal lover, I wondered if the energy healing would help them feel better . . . and whether the results would be noticeable given that there is no placebo effect with animals. Were they ever! The results, however, varied: some were subtle, positive changes; others were miraculous. Most animals showed immediate visible results after only one session. It was quickly evident that conducting sessions on animals must have always been part of my life's plan. Working with animals soon became a vital component of my healing practice. The contributions that animals have made to humankind's evolution are unrivaled, so I consider it an honor to serve them in this way.

TANDEM HEALING SESSIONS

During my early work with animals, I identified the many levels of animal-human mirroring in any given animal-human relationship. It was fascinating to learn that animals mirror the same unhealed emotional wound(s) as their person. For example, they might both have an unhealed abandonment wound. Left to its own devices, the emotional wound is likely to manifest as a needy, codependent relationship, and the animal might exhibit moderate to severe separation anxiety when not with its human guardian.

The lion's share of the time, when people schedule an appointment for their animal, they aren't necessarily thinking about what their animal could be mirroring or carrying for them in that moment. I get it! Animal lovers are rightfully motivated to take action to alleviate any source of discomfort or suffering in their beloved companions.

Nevertheless, when a person is proactively on their own inner healing journey, their animals have fewer issues and their behavioral and physical wounds heal faster. After I facilitate an animal's healing session, I share energetic observations with their human to give them another level of insight into their animal's issue . . . some of which might be reflecting the same issues that their person has. Frequently when I reveal details of an animal's session, their human will have an aha moment and mention the parallels in themselves. For example, if I disclose that I feel dense energy releasing from a specific area of an animal's body, the person might respond that they themselves have a physical issue in the same area.

It is a pivotal relationship-changing moment when a person begins to see and believe in the healing alliance they have with their animal companion. This modification in perspective and new level of awareness activates an immediate shift of energy within them both, such that the relationship will never be the same again.

In general animals tend to heal at an accelerated rate due to their trust in the organic nature of healing through the energy field. When documenting the results of various animal sessions I've conducted, I noticed something interesting. Often a person would tell me that, following a session, their animal's negative behavior had completely stopped or their physical issue had healed, only to contact me days, weeks, or months later stating it had returned, or a new ailment or negative behavior had suddenly presented itself. In those and other cases I wondered whether the animal might completely heal, and whether the healing results would stick *if* their person was engaged in doing their inner work alongside them.

What if I connected simultaneously to both the animal *and* the person? Would their mutually shared wounds heal faster? Since some animals are more sensitive and therefore more apt to absorb their person's emotional energy, would the energy and emotions be released more easily during a mutual session? I decided it was time to find out the answer to these questions. I was hopeful that both the person and the animal would benefit, and that their capacity to heal would be accelerated by their mutual commitment to that goal.

Hence a new level of fascinating research and learnings commenced with my new Tandem Healings service offering. For the research sessions I requested that a four-session commitment be completed over a four- to six-week period of time. The findings were unique within each animal-human pairing.

At the completion of their series of sessions, most of the individuals felt a stronger bond with their animal, as well as a deeper understanding of the higher purpose and plan they had agreed upon with their animal. Many times the healing results were palpable and very profound—beyond what I had anticipated or hoped could transpire.

Later in the book, you'll get to meet Rick and his dog Sammie. Sammie wandered onto Rick's farm one day as a stray—hungry and fearful. Rick had one very firm intention for their Tandem Healing sessions: to heal the codependency in his relationship with Sammie so his beloved dog could be more independent and less needy. As early as the first session, Rick suddenly became aware of Sammie's behavior mirroring his own codependency needs, which he'd exhibited in every "love" relationship he'd had in his entire life. He also realized the higher purpose of his mutual healing journey with his wonderful dog, who, at a soul level, had sought him out so they could heal *together*.

Lynn and her beloved dog Sophie were another human-animal team whose story moved me deeply. In two years, Lynn had three dogs unexpectantly pass, right before her husband of thirty-three years went into cardiopulmonary crisis and collapsed on their dining room floor, gasping for his last breath. The paramedics were delayed by traffic, and upon their arrival they were unable to save him. Lynn signed up to receive Tandem Healing sessions, hoping to release her grief, as well as help Sophie release hers. She wanted both of their hearts to heal, and she was also hoping for a miracle. Her beloved dog, Sophie, had just unexpectedly been diagnosed with a strong heart murmur. This was a condition that the veterinarian warned might lead to a condition that was similar to her husband's.

These remarkable accounts, in addition to many more divinely orchestrated animal-human Tandem Healings documented in chapter 5, "Tandem Healing Case Studies," will give you insights into the soul agreements that can lovingly be held in the center of *your* sacred animal partnerships.

SOUL CHAT ROOM

As you read this book, I periodically refer to a soul chat room. It's been termed a *soul chat room* by yours truly, because that perfectly describes its activities. During healing sessions, I became aware of a bubble of bright white light above me, and within it were two souls communicating. I intuitively knew that one of the souls was the Higher Self of the person or animal I was energetically connected to for the healing session. The second soul in the soul chat room is typically significant to my client's healing process.

The Higher Self is the part of our soul that is the highest aspect of ourselves. When we tune in to our hearts for inner guidance we are in essence communicating with our Higher Self. It is also commonly referred to as an oversoul, or I AM Presence. Our Higher Self remembers everything that our 3-D human (and animal) incarnate identity has intentionally forgotten. For example, our Higher Self holds wisdom about our contracts and soul agreements with each being in our life.

Sometimes I am privy to what's being discussed in the soul chat room. Other times I get a knowing about the topic and sense the feelings between the two beings.

Frequently the message from the soul chat room is one confirming that the Higher Selves of the animal and human know each other. The message may also contain an acknowledgment that they intentionally designed their lives to intersect for the higher purpose of their mutual development. I often perceive that both souls have teamed up for each other's growth multiple times. And in every soul chat room that shows up in the healing sessions, there is a distinct knowing that their encounter on the physical plane, however brief, is rooted in unconditional love.

Michael & Maddie

Recently I was at my office facilitating a healing session on a person when suddenly I noticed a soul chat room above me. I immediately recognized that it was the Higher Self of a different client, Michael, and his beloved senior terrier, Maddie. Earlier that morning Michael had accidentally tripped and fallen on top of Maddie. I had been told prior to going to the office that Michael and his wife, Kathy, had rushed Maddie to the vet after the incident, but I hadn't yet heard the outcome.

In the soul chat room, Maddie's Higher Self was thanking Michael for agreeing to help her out of her body. She was showering him with love and gratitude. Maddie was glowing with brilliant white and golden light and was very happy to be back "home." At my first available moment, I reached out to Kathy for an update on Maddie. She confirmed that they had released Maddie back to Spirit and that Michael was in deep anguish and taking it very hard, blaming himself for the incident.

From the moment the couple had rescued Maddie, she and Michael had formed a deep connection. Even though they knew upon adopting her that Maddie was a senior girl with several health issues, no animal lover wants to be responsible for their pet's passing before they are ready to go. Every animal lover can imagine the pain Michael must have felt when the accident happened.

When I shared with Kathy and Michael what I'd observed in the soul chat room it brought them much relief. I disclosed how Michael's and Maddie's Higher Selves had planned the incident, and told them that Michael's soul had bravely chosen to help Maddie return to Spirit. This truly was an incredibly loving and courageous

Michael and Maddie

choice that Michael's soul had made, knowing the potential pain it would inflict upon his human self.

Maddie had always been very independent and had never been a lapdog. Michael mentioned that in her last few days she had finally been ready to allow more love in, and for the first time, she'd leaned into his love for her, asking him to pet her. This must have been part of her healing contract with Michael. His unconditional love and care helped her to open her heart such that it fulfilled their soul contract.

Forever Connected

While connected to a dog during a healing session, I observed a gentleman speaking with the Higher Self of my canine client in a soul chat room. He was talking about a behavior to amend to help the dog have less anxiety. The man had been the dog's guardian before he (the man) had passed. It was incredible to see the continuation of their connection after the man had transitioned, and while the dog was still living. The gentleman was so patient, loving, and kind to the dog. Watching them together opened *my* heart. When I shared the conversation with my client after the dog's session, she said it was no surprise that her husband would still be guiding and coaching their dog from the other side. They apparently had exactly that type of relationship when together on the physical plane.

May you find peace in knowing that your Higher Self is actively engaged in soul talk with all those you are in relationship with, including your light team on the other side. The intention of these conversations is to collaborate with those you love to manifest the type of experiences you desire for your personal growth.

YOUR LIGHT TEAM

Early in my ability to see into other dimensions, I was surprised and comforted to learn that we all have beings of light around us for guidance and support. And it's a full-time gig! Indeed, there are high-vibrating, wise, and loving beings that are *always* around us and available to us to lean into for support. Our light teams' unconditional love for us is undeniable—much like that of our animal companions.

These extraordinary light beings are more commonly known as spirit guides, though many simply call them angels. I refer to them as "the beings of light who work with me."

There are typically one to three light beings with you all the time, and reinforcements instantaneously show up as needed during difficult times or when you call upon them. Your light team is especially close to you during a healing session, providing support, guidance, and nurturance. The unconditional love and acceptance they feel for you is undeniable and endlessly flows from their being to yours. They know and love every fiber of your being and admire your courage to embrace this roller coaster of a human ride.

You contracted with your spirit guides in advance of your birth and have undoubtedly known, loved, and learned from your specific team for a very long time. This is a very intimate, loving, respectful, and sacred relationship.

Be proactive in your quest to connect with them. Sometimes they need your permission to intervene, so I encourage you to actively enlist their guidance. I recall when my cat Sundance swallowed the rubber cap of a toy, and by the time I realized what had happened she was turning blue and lying motionless on the bed. I knew there wasn't enough time to get her to the veterinarian, so I beckoned the beings of light who work with me. I asked them to help her (more like begged). I was beside myself. Instantaneously Sundance began moving and then regurgitating. She sat up, and out of her mouth popped the cap. Just like that.

Small and large miracles happen every single day of your life. Becoming aware of them will pave the way for countless more to magically unfold. Engaging with your team is highly recommended if you want to allow more unforgettable, mind-blowing, synchronistic moments into your life.

You might find it especially interesting that animals that share their lives with people, or live in nature, also have spirit guides. These guides are frequently elemental beings, or various other types of animal allies such as past animal pals, angels, and sometimes the spirits of people who are serving animals.

*The light teams of the person and their animal
work together harmoniously for the
benefit of them both.*

Your Loved Ones

People or animals that have previously passed can and will also
be there for you as needed. They are not usually part of your
light team, but it's possible. It depends on how long it has been
since they've passed—as they need time to recalibrate once back
on the other side. However, they are and always will be available
for you to connect with as needed, as the following story of mine
will illustrate.

My sister and I were helping our father move out of his
home and into an assisted living center during the worst real
estate market in my lifetime. His home was in Phoenix, Arizona,
which at the time had the poorest home sales market in the
nation. The house wasn't yet on the market, and the local real
estate professionals I consulted were worried about its salabil-
ity in a down market. I tried to detach from the well-intended
guidance: they strongly recommended that I turn his home into
a rental home, then list it during a better economic time.

For the first time since my mother had passed eight years
prior, I decided to engage with her through consistent prayer,
asking for her assistance for a quick and prosperous sale of
their home. It was my personal experiment to ask for her help
with a project that would be easy to gauge the outcome of.
During this time, she was the only being I called upon for
assistance, mainly because of her personal connection to the
home. I also prayed that the buyers would be a family that
would truly love and appreciate the home.

The home sold the first day on the market—*above* the
asking price. The buyers, a kind young couple with a new

baby, were also interested in procuring the entire contents of our father's shed, including tools and lawn mower. They also purchased some of his furniture. The entire process couldn't have gone more smoothly!

Animal Council

All animal and nature lovers, and especially people who work with animals in any capacity, have animal totems and an animal council that provides them with support and guidance. This is yet another level of knowledge that I highly suggest you learn more about. There are many books on the subject; the numerous books of the late Ted Andrews in particular resonate with me.

You might already be aware of the animal totem assigned to you at birth. If you're drawn to a certain species of animal, that would be a big clue. For example, I've had many wonderful dreams wherein a beautiful golden lioness visits me, and I've also had a deep fascination with elephants. My home is decorated with many paintings and sculptures of elephants. These are indications that I'm connecting with the energy of both the lioness and elephant in this life to integrate their teachings.

You are surrounded with a bevy of light beings that have so got your back.

When you consciously begin to develop an intimate heart-to-heart relationship with the beings of light who work with you, the more they can and will be of service. They aspire to support your growth and lighten your load. When you tune in to them, they will feel familiar to your soul, much like your animals do. Intentionally connect with your spirit guides and consciously allow their love to flow into your heart. If you make that a practice for five minutes each day, it can be life-changing. Even better, you will no longer feel alone in a large, sometimes frightening universe. You become linked to Spirit and feel a kinship with the whole of Creation.

THE PLAN

At a soul level people and animals have agreed to join forces to advance their souls' objectives to heal, evolve, serve, and allow in more love. Upon birth each being forgets the vast and unlimited knowledge held in the palm of their soul's hand and begins adapting to their earthly experience. All souls are aware of the divergence of energy on our planet, and yet they still courageously choose to incarnate for this experience of communal growth and healing.

Regardless of the experiences you've consciously or unconsciously planned, everything you and your animals have gone through has one desired end result: to love, to know love, to feel love, to give love, and to *be* love. Yes, it *is* easier said than done in a world that reflects the opposite of love at every turn. But without the contrast of fear-based emotions, you would not appreciate, know, and feel love as deeply and intimately as you do.

The familiar and deep love you feel for your animals is palpable for a reason. There is literally a cord of energy connecting your hearts. This is one reason why you intuitively know their preferences and desires better than anyone else, and especially so when making big decisions on their behalf.

This light-filled cord enables love and wellness to flow between you both, which is a strong motivation to maintain good self-care. It is also the reason you are aware when something's off with them and vice versa. The love between you is endless, and the bond is like no other.

The animal kingdom has collectively raised their paws, wings, and fins, and exclaimed that they are more than willing to serve humanity by helping them remember the truth and beauty of who they are, even if that means showing compassion to people that many would deem unlovable. Animal lovers are fortunate to have these beautiful creatures in their lives as partners, mirrors, and messengers of the Divine.

SACRED INSIGHTS

Animals are always modeling a way of being more mindful. They are subtly inviting you to join them.

If you are someone who tends to open your heart and get emotionally closer to animals more so than to people, then animals will undoubtedly be paramount to your growth here in Earth School. Consciously partnering with your animal teachers is key to you both having fewer physical and behavioral issues.

Once you identify and work with the soul agreements you have created with your animals, every experience with them takes on fresh new meaning. You will never look at them through the same lens again! They are your willing soul partners on this sometimes turbulent, sometimes peaceful ride called *life*. The awareness of your soul's reciprocal plan enables more love to flow between you, and then to others, which lights the way for all beings you encounter.

2

The Sacred Transition
of the Animal Soul

Animal lovers are extraordinary in that they are aware of the looming probability that they will outlive their beloved pets. Yet they are still drawn, time and time again, to the connection, the teachings, and the joy that is uniquely special to sharing their lives, homes, and laps with animals. They choose love over the fear of the emotional pain that is sure to come with the eventual loss. For most animal guardians, their loving companion's final days and moments are some of the most difficult and painful experiences of their lives.

This topic is fresh on my heart. In 2018 my long-term cat companions, MaiTai and Sundance, whom I was sharing my life with when I wrote *Soul Healing with Our Animal Companions*, passed away within a few months of each other right before the book's release. What I have experienced through my practice helped me to more easily lean into the process with my two cats, to intentionally and lovingly create extraordinary and sacred transitions for them.

It is with great intention and hope that sharing what I have learned will help you to create, when possible, a sacred final chapter for *your* animals. Or at the minimum, an easier process for you when they pass, so you will have less fear around their impending transition. This will greatly enhance your animal's experience.

Often I am hired to facilitate healing sessions on animals during their last months, days, hours, or even during the very moment of a veterinarian-assisted euthanasia. Early in my practice I learned that I would frequently work with animals during this sacred time at the end of their life. It's a common and natural time for people to reach out for help since they want to find a way to help their animal feel better and be more comfortable, or determine if their pet is suffering or in pain. Over the years I've learned that my ability to show up for people and their animals during this period of their lives must have always been part of the bigger plan for me.

As any person or animal nears the end of its life, bioenergetic healings serve a deeper, more divine purpose: they prepare the soul to exit the body through the crown chakra, located at the top of the head. These healing sessions are usually very productive, and embedded within them is a strong sense of higher purpose. These sessions can also include the practice of releasing energetic codependency cords, as well as energy and emotions that have been absorbed from others—in addition to *any* energetic congestion that the animal would prefer to release while still in its body. Once they have left their body temple, this healing work shortens their adjustment period on the other side.

It is truly an honor to be part of this incredible moment when a soul leaves the body and returns to the spirit realm. In a way, it's a graduation upward and forward to the next chapter of their soul's evolution, where they will be free and can better support their beloved person(s). Each time I hold that sacred space, it is indescribable and profoundly moving. To be able to sense the beauty and splendor of the soul's release is something I feel very honored to witness. The amount of pure and unconditional angelic love that surrounds the animals and their people during these final moments leaves me with a renewed sense of peace. Just knowing that we are always supported, that there is always loving energy around us—but especially so during the more difficult times—reinforces my belief that every soul continues its journey.

Sharing with you what I see and feel during healing sessions conducted with animals near transition to Spirit will raise your awareness. It will also give you insights into what is simultaneously happening in the other dimensions, so that *your* recovery and healing process may be softened before and after your animal returns to Spirit. Below I share with you some of what I have observed during healing sessions that are conducted when animals are nearing or going through their transition time:

- There is a very strong high vibrational angelic presence that surrounds the animal and the people who love him or her. The angels and spirit guides are there for you to lean into for comfort and support. They also surround you, your pet, and your family with a strong, protective boundary because fearful times can draw in lower vibrations. You can ask this angelic presence to help you find clarity and to release your fears, pain, and worries. Intentionally connect with these light beings heart-to-heart to feel their unconditional love. During the release of your companion's soul, the amount of angelic, pure love around the animal and their guardian(s) intensifies.

- There is a beautiful balancing, cleansing, and opening of the crown chakra (at the top of the head) to ease the release of the animal's soul, and a spectacular golden white light reaching down from above. This light has the feel and sensation of a magnet, which eases the soul up and out of the body when it's the animal's time to leave.

- Energetic heart chakra cords connect us with everyone we are, or ever have been, in relationship with. During these healing sessions, I frequently notice that the heart chakra relationship cord is cleansed and purified between the animal and the people who have given permission for this cleansing. Permission can be given consciously, usually when you have come to a place of peace about releasing your animal back to Spirit. The heart chakra cord between the two of you remains tethered even after your animal has left their body, which makes it easier for you to continue sensing and connecting with them.

- Your Higher Self, (the highest aspect of the soul) greets your animal when they transition. On every occasion that I've witnessed this, the person's own Higher Self was glowing and beaming with love, pride, and gratitude—smiling and completely at peace while simultaneously offering a warm *welcome home* to them.

- People and animals you'd hoped would greet your animal when they transition will be there to welcome your pet. You can trust that your request for this to happen has been heard. Each time I've described to a client who I observed greeting their animal, they've responded by telling me that they had prayed, asked for, or hoped that this specific person (or animal) would be the one to greet their animal after its transition.

- Immediately after the animal's soul has moved out of its

body, I've witnessed very sacred honoring by the masters and beings of light that work with you and your animal. It is as if they are in ceremony or holding space for the passing of your pet. They provide a strong and sacred light of protection around the animal and their people. Frequently they are in a circle and sometimes are down on one knee with heads tipped forward honorably. Other times there is a feeling of celebration, with light beings and fairies dancing in a circle. I cannot imagine a better welcome home ceremony, which honors the life of teachings and love that animals provide. I've noticed that there is a personal connection to the type of honoring circle, and it has to do with the beliefs, personality, and sacred work of the animal and their person(s).

- There's a possibility the animal's soul will pass through their person when or after they leave their body, which is an act of gratitude and love. You might sense this as a whoosh of energy or you may experience tingles. Everyone is different in how they sense energy, and there are endless ways for your pet to reach out to you once they are on the other side. But if you think you felt something, you probably did, and it was most likely their soul.

- The animal's human guardian might receive a "heart-fusion" greeting after the animal's soul exits their body. *Heart fusion* is how I am choosing to describe an extraordinary, high-vibration soul-to-soul greeting. It's the union of two souls fusing at the heart. It is a euphoric feeling in which you will feel and recall your soul's familiarity with the deep love you have for each other, and you will feel intensified levels of gratitude, love, and joy. Perhaps this is a common practice that two souls on the other side utilize to express intimacy and love for each other. I've only felt this twice and will never forget it. It feels like ecstasy and brought immediate tears of joy to my eyes and a strong intimate *knowing* of the other soul.

Family Love for Rosco

One day I received an urgent call from an emotional client, Jim, who was at the veterinarian's office with his senior dog Rosco, contemplating making the difficult choice to help his beloved dog end his suffering. Jim was surprised by his emotions when speaking to me, but I could tell he knew it was Rosco's time. He asked me what I have experienced about an animal's preference to be either in the vet's office or at home when they pass. I told him that I could not know, as he would be able to, what Rosco's personal preference would be. I added that, when possible, I've learned that most animals prefer to be at home with their family when they transition.

As far as I'm concerned, nothing is more difficult than making a life-altering decision about an animal companion that has been nothing less than one of God's greatest and best gifts in our life. And when the synchronicities line up, like the events with this client's dog did, you have no doubt that there is a higher power involved, orchestrating every detail. Jim decided to take Rosco home and, together with his wife and children, spend some time saying goodbye.

His veterinarian was available to facilitate an in-home euthanasia later that afternoon. Jim asked me to facilitate one last energy healing session prior to the vet's visit. During the session, it would be family time and final goodbyes. He didn't want his young children to witness the actual euthanasia.

My schedule miraculously cleared to be able to facilitate a remote healing session on Rosco to prepare him for the veterinarian-assisted transition directly afterward. The healing session was Rosco's final gift from "his dad." The entire family surrounded their beloved dog with love, expressing gratitude to him during the healing session, saying their painful goodbyes and weeping, sharing stories and telling Rosco how much they loved him.

Hours earlier Rosco thought he might be saying goodbye at the vet's office, perhaps not where he preferred to be, though where he no doubt would have been lovingly taken care of. Instead, he manifested being able to be home with his beloved family. Toward the end of the session, when I was just about to disconnect, I followed my intuitive guidance and stayed connected to Rosco for five minutes more.

I'm so glad I did because they were the most incredible five minutes! I felt an amazing and gentle release of energy from Rosco's crown chakra, saw a bevy of angels surrounding the family, and became aware of a very high vibration of love and light easily flowing through Rosco. It was in every way a sacred and beautiful moment to witness as his soul released from his body. His soul felt so happy and free.

This wonderful dog was literally in the hands of his loving family when he took his last breath, which is just where he wanted to be. In this, the children learned that it is safe to bear witness to the natural unfolding and ending of life. And the experience of this sacred event allowed the family to share something that they will forever remember. Through all the emotions that flowed from their heartbreak, they supported each other through each tear. There is beauty in everything, even in endings.

The type of energy healing session that I performed on Rosco can release any congested energy and aid in a natural passing. The sessions will consistently help the animal to move forward in the highest and best way possible, whatever path that is. Sometimes that means they continue their life journey feeling better, and at other times it helps the animal prepare for their time to return to Spirit.

I always share the possibility (of the soul leaving) with

people prior to conducting healings sessions when the animal is especially close to the end of its journey in this life. On rare occasions, as with Rosco, I've been connected to an animal, and it gently and beautifully passed during the session. Animal lovers always hope for an easy and gentle passing for their pets, and I have learned that it is a blessing for all when that occurs. The animals would not leave without choosing to do so at the soul level. And each time I've been connected to an animal and their soul unexpectedly released from their body, their *person* had already given the animal permission to leave. Both beings were unattached to the outcome of the session and were emotionally ready for the animal's departure.

MaiTai's Final Gift

My beloved cat companion, MaiTai, was eighteen years young and still the light of my life. Our bond was strong, and we were deeply connected with an enhanced sense of soul familiarity and intimacy. I do not know how many lives we have been through together, or if he is even from my soul group, but my guess would be that we have loved one another for a very long time. We all have love connections with many souls. However, we will get a more intimate and familiar feeling with those with whom we've created a strong bond through sharing many lives. These souls are said to be part of our soul group.

MaiTai's health had been deteriorating for about a year and a half, and I knew that without the one medication I gave him every three to four days, he would suffer and begin the transitioning process. My personal goal was to receive clarity around assisting him back to Spirit, with his permission, just ahead of the curve, so that his last moments would not be in an emergency room experiencing a heightened level of pain and suffering.

There wasn't anything I ever wished for or asked of him that didn't unfold just as I'd hoped. He was a nurturer and very stoic. I had gotten him as a kitten just after the turn of the twenty-first century. In the previous months, my mother and all three of my cat companions had transitioned. A criterion of my selection process was that I receive an obvious sign from the kitten I was to be with. So I went to a place where there was a roomful of kittens to adopt and decided I would only get the one that, when I picked it up, didn't claw or squirm to get out of my arms. And most importantly, when I looked into the kitten's eyes, I asked that he or she would give me a slow blink so I would recognize it as the one I should take home with me. Cats are very expressive with their eyes, and a slow blink is always an expression of love. I'll have you know that MaiTai was the last kitten in the room that I picked up, and he gave me a beautiful slow blink.

On the night before he transitioned, he was lying on my lap, and I began talking to him about whether he was ready to "go" or not. I told him I would honor whatever he wanted, and if he preferred to stay in the (for lack of a better term) hospice care that I'd been giving him, I would lovingly do that until he told my heart it was his time to leave. During this conversation, he was looking into my eyes, listening intently, understanding every single word I was saying. So I asked him, "Are you ready to go back home?" He then unexpectedly and lovingly gave me one long slow blink. I gasped with surprise and immediately began crying, knowing that his soul remembered how to let me know his wishes.

Exchanging slow blinks wasn't one of our games or regular things we did to talk with each other. But there he was, giving me the exact same signal that had brought us together. There was no doubt in my heart or mind what had transpired between us during that conversation. I reached out to a wonderful Lap of Love veterinarian I knew, Dr. Lauren Cassady. (Lap of Love offers in-home geriatric care and euthanasia services.) We set up a time for the very next day with her available veterinarian, Dr. Ashley Payne, to come to my house to help MaiTai move on to the next chapter of his soul's journey.

I decided to write MaiTai a poem of gratitude that I would read and create an altar featuring his favorite toys, my favorite photos of him, a candle, and a few other small, meaningful items.

From the moment Dr. Ashley arrived, I know that MaiTai knew exactly what was happening because our connection was so strong. Even though my heart was breaking, I found the inner strength and courage to honor him and make his last moments meaningful for us both.

The time had arrived for the doctor to help MaiTai get his wings. I'd said my final words and honored him in the way I felt he deserved. The barrier of light and love that surrounded us, filled with so many angelic beings, was amazing and something I will never forget. MaiTai was lying on my lap, and Dr. Ashley was lovingly

Tammy and MaiTai

administering to him. Because of his age there was a bit of finagling and difficulty finding an active vein for his final injection. Instead of focusing on that, I decided to close my eyes and take deep breaths and send him love and a knowing that he would easily release and soon be free. I wanted to comfort *both* of us, and this helped.

With my eyes still closed, a minute or two later, I felt his soul release. Then MaiTai gifted me with a euphoric soul-honoring heart fusion (like I described earlier). Tears were streaming down my face, and I sat in awe of this incredible last gift of love and gratitude from his soul. It lasted about ten seconds. Without opening my eyes, I said in not more than a whisper to Dr. Ashley, who was patiently allowing me to just *be* in the moment with my experience, "I'm assuming you found a vein that worked." She replied, "Yes." I said my goodbyes to MaiTai's physical presence, and Dr. Ashley wrapped him in a beautiful blanket and laid him in a basket. He looked so peaceful.

There are many people who believe animals prefer to live until the day their bodies die naturally on their own. I believe that the animals that are with those people wanted and agreed to have that experience, at some level, or they wouldn't be together. It could also be that the person is picking up those wishes from the animal. Regardless, it's important to trust your heart connection with your animal for the right and perfect ending to its life. You can trust your connection to your animal to guide you with any big decisions you must make on its behalf. If finances prohibit your desires, there are nonprofits or veterinarians that sometimes offer financial assistance for their services.

Lily's Conscious Ceremony

I'd been working regularly with Anyaa's dog Lily for nearly three years when it was her time to transition back to Spirit. Lily and

Anyaa had an incredibly deep soul bond. It was abundantly clear from Lily's first healing sessions that they'd been together for many lifetimes, and my sense was that Lily was from Anyaa's soul group. We all have soul groups, which some call our "soul tribe," which we frequently incarnate with to help each other evolve, grow, release karma, and love more deeply. I believe that in certain instances one member of our soul tribe can incarnate as an animal to work with us and teach us one of the Pinnacle Teachings. (There will be more on the Pinnacle Teachings in chapter 4, "Types of Soul Contracts Defined.") Anyaa and Lily were a dynamic healing team, and groups of women went through Anyaa's healing program globally. Lily's last years were miracles, for she'd had a couple of medical issues that her veterinarian had thought would end her life much earlier.

In the next to last distance healing session I facilitated on Lily, I was shown a visual of Anyaa's Higher Self dressed in all white, opening a gate to receive Lily. Her face was glowing, and she was filled with peace and unconditional love. I contemplated whether to share the image as I knew it meant that it was very close to Lily's time, and the decision of an animal's transition time should come directly from their guardian. This was the first time I became aware of the guardian's Higher Self greeting their animal's soul. Throughout my years of working with Lily, I knew that at the minimum, she was an evolved master healer. Her soul would pop into my sessions as part of my healing team with clients while she was still in her body and many times after she returned to the other side. I consider her one of my greatest teachers, and she will always be near and dear to my heart.

Anyaa lives in an all-intentional community in the mountains of North Carolina. She asked me to formally connect to Lily at the exact moment that she, with the aid of their local holistic veterinarian, returned to Spirit. As I described earlier, a healing session can ease the animal's passing to enable their soul to release from their body and adjust to the other side once there.

Anyaa describes the conscious ceremony she created to honor Lily's life of service and love.

"Miss Lily was a very social girl, and not only loved to greet my clients and students but had to say good-bye to all her favorite places, people, and dogs before she left. A few days before her passing, I took her with me as was usual, to the opening circle of a Wise Wolf Women's Council in my community. There were about a hundred women in the circle, and Lily went around the entire circle and acknowledged everyone. She often did this in my much smaller circles, but *this* was extraordinary. It was Friday. I had no idea at the time that we would decide that the following Wednesday was her day to return to Spirit.

Lily and Anyaa McAndrew, M.A., LPC, NCC,
transpersonal shamanic psychotherapist

"The day she and I decided was her time to go, we took one last walk up her favorite trail, and as weak as she was, she was very determined to do the whole thing, straight uphill. We then went to visit her dog friends Anubis and Vision. Then she led me to the front yard of our community retreat center where she laid down in the grass. We enjoyed watching the birds and squirrels together, and when she was complete, we made our way back to our house to await the time of the ceremony.

"Tammy and Lily and I had been working together for three years when my new beloved, Gary, had just recently moved from Seattle to western North Carolina so we could begin our life together. We all had the distinct feeling that Lily knew I would be okay now that Gary had arrived. I got the sense that Lily's knowledge that I would be supported helped her feel better about leaving her body. It was literally six days after Gary arrived when we had her sacred ceremony.

"There were at least twenty people gathered to honor Lily and see her off. In addition, my holistic vet, Dr. Tami Shearer, came to administer the drug, and Tammy Billups was on the phone to help Lily out of her body. My friend Anne held a large quartz crystal at Lily's third eye to assist her. It was the most difficult decision of my life, but I knew beyond a doubt that assisting her departure in this way was the right thing to do.

"It's interesting that I always felt that Lily contained at least an aspect of a daughter that I never had. Before I got her as a puppy, I felt a girl child (soul) around me but the energy was not strong enough in me or in my marriage at the time to bring in a child.

"I miss Lily so much, and tears still gather in my eyes when I talk about her ten years later. She was a heavenly gift, and the love of my life for fifteen wonderful years."

Are Your Soul Contracts Completed?

At a soul level, you and your animal companion are very aware of what you are helping each other learn and why you signed up to mutually heal. Much of the time, your animal friend will stay in its body until your soul contracts have been completed. Sometimes, even if your soul contract is completed, they'll stay with you until you have allowed another love (person, baby, or animal) into your life. At this point, they might choose to manifest a physical ailment or another way to leave the body. They may choose to stay until you give yourself permission to move forward and allow a new love into your life; then they might quickly exit.

Many times people are inadvertently confused by this and think they may have caused the early departure of their pet by having opened their heart to love another person or animal, and unknowingly blame themselves. Please know that your animal was simply waiting for you to have another love in your life first. Send them gratitude and know it was all divinely orchestrated for your highest good.

When an animal has a quick release or you must make a decision on their behalf that seems to come out of nowhere, know that this is also predestined and part of your soul contract. If things began moving in a direction that is not aligned with that of your prearranged soul contract, they might choose to leave and come back at another time. Every soul has free will.

Let's say you had a pet that developed a sudden illness that ended its life at a young age. It might be that your soul contract was already completed. Or perhaps your soul contract was to have the animal pass early so you could learn something through its passing. Maybe you become an advocate to raise awareness about the illness that ended its life, or it helped you tap into unexpressed grief from prior unresolved losses.

Many people have had unfortunate years full of multiple losses, which could include the loss of a home, job, animal, or loved one(s). Ultimately, this can be a catalyst to embrace a new way of being that is in their highest and best interest. My spiritual journey began with my mother's passing, followed by the passing of my three beloved cats within months. I knew without a doubt that even in the midst of the most difficult year of my life, they were ready to transition, for our contracts had been for them to support me up until that time and no further. They were carrying a lot of my "stuff," so while it was a difficult time, I was glad they were no longer suffering. They each taught me so much about myself. Experiencing their loving gifts helped me to feel in ways I had never felt before.

Similarly, my father passed almost eighteen years after my mother and the cats I shared my life with at that time transitioned within months afterward. Things don't always happen this way, but they can. The second time it was much easier because all three of them that had passed had lived long, healthy, loving lives, and I was much healthier emotionally and physically. But I knew, much like when my mother passed, that I had entered a new phase of my life and that I would be okay. I was very clear that our soul contracts were completed, and that we'll be back together again.

In the middle of difficult years, or times that include multiple losses, know that these periods hold much beauty and growth for your soul. You have learned what these light beams, *your animal companions, came to teach so that you can move forward, better for what they have showed you about yourself.*

Jasmine's Surprising Message

There's a well-known term often used in animal rescue that describes Jasmine. Jasmine is a "foster failure." Jeff was volunteering for an animal rescue organization, helping with adoptions one Saturday in 2003, when he got wind of a rescued Lab mix that had given birth to thirteen puppies underneath a mobile home in a trailer park. He immediately responded to help the fur family. The puppies quickly found their forever homes, which left the strong mother, now named Jasmine, up for adoption.

Jeff and his wife, Gigi, fostered Jasmine and for many months took her to weekend adoption events to help her find a forever home, until one day they suddenly realized she already had one.

Jasmine had a wonderful life for sixteen additional years. She was always a healthy and vigorous girl until March of 2019 when she lost the use of her back legs. Fortunately Jeff worked from home, which allowed him to keep a close eye on Jasmine as she lay on her bed next to his desk. Despite her physical limitations, she still had a voracious appetite, was clear of mind, and even desired to play. She showed no signs of wanting to "leave." Frequently Jeff told Jasmine that he would happily carry her around as long as he continued to get clear messages that it wasn't her time.

During this period of loving dependency, their bond strengthened even more. Jeff began to *sense* when she needed to go outside. Sometimes when he was in the shower or at the grocery store, he'd suddenly get the feeling that Jasmine needed him, and, always accurate and in tune with his girl, he'd rush to her side.

Five months into their new routine things began to change, and Jeff called to set up a session with me. Jasmine wasn't as interested in eating and seemed to have lost that spark in her eye. More than that, their around-the-clock routine was really wearing on Jeff. He kept a camera on her constantly, and it was all getting to be very physically and emotionally challenging.

Shortly after connecting heart-to-heart with Jasmine for her healing session, I noticed she was trying to show me something through my mind's eye. I could see the back of a woman with dark hair standing and talking on a cell phone. Then all of a sudden I heard the woman say a portion of a sentence with utmost clarity: "the soul contracts are completed."

Hearing this I gasped; not because of the words but because I recognized that the voice and woman was *me*. Jasmine had taken me to a conversation I'd had with a friend the previous week. I'd vehemently shared with my friend that if I were ever bedridden, and the soul contracts with my caretakers had been completed, I'd rather be helped out of my body than watch those I loved struggle while tending to me.

Jeff and Jasmine

I believe this was Jasmine's way of relaying that her heart was breaking watching her beloved person struggle while caring for her, and that their soul contracts were completed. After sharing with Jeff what Jasmine had shown me, he broke down and wept, the words ringing true. "Yes of course," he said. "That would be Jasmine, worried about me more than about herself."

After a lengthy discussion, Jeff and Gigi made the decision to move forward to assist their beloved Jasmine back to Spirit. Their veterinarian was available to come to their home the next day, and it was a very sacred and peaceful passing. Jeff shared that he felt peace in his soul with the decision. He knew in his heart that this was what Jasmine wanted.

Animals are very aware of everything you are feeling, and it can be difficult for them to observe your struggles. It is never easy to see any being we love suffer emotional and physical challenges. And yet Jasmine's story teaches us that there are times when an animal will find a way to give you permission to assist in their passing because your shared experiences are no longer serving your mutual evolution, and the soul contracts are complete.

SACRED INSIGHTS

The joy, unconditional love, acceptance, and endless teachings from the light beams we call our pets draw us in like a magnet. We learn that we have the courage within to open our hearts to share our lives with them again and again, because the love and comfort animals bring into our lives is incomparable. Love is worth it. Love is to be cherished and beholden. Our souls already know this. Love is why we are here, and it's imperative for our soul's growth. If you believe as I do that this isn't your first incarnation, then you are already a step ahead in the ability to find peace after your pet transitions to the other side. Your belief that the soul is everlasting, and the knowing that you will see each other again—maybe even in your current lifetime—will aid you in your healing process.

There's nothing worse than the thought of your animal suffering in any way. That thought, in and of itself, creates suffering and fear in the people who love them. Combine that with unreleased pain from past losses and it snowballs into a heightened level of anxiety and fear around losing your animal. The part of you that intimately knows and fears feeling emotional pain wants to protect your heart and put a lock and key on being vulnerable. Another name for this syndrome is called "being human." However, if the part of you that fears losing your animal is in control of your decisions on its behalf, you might be missing out on some tender, sacred, honoring final moments with your beloved animal companion, or perhaps even missing their messages about their preferences.

Animals do not fear death. They know it is a part of life and that you'll be together still, just in another way. It's important for people to work on their attachment (to a specific outcome) and give themselves permission to have good self-care during their animal's last months, weeks, and days. This enables them to more easily hold sacred space and make choices from the adult part of themselves that feels the heart-to-heart connection with their pet.

Remember, no one knows your animal better than you do. While making the decision to help them leave their body is by far one of *the* hardest decisions you will ever make, you will have peace when you tune in to the heart connection you already have with your animal, trusting your heart to guide you. Sometimes nurturing the child within yourself is needed before you can have a clearer connection of trust in what you are sensing.

Trusting yourself and your heart connection with your animal to make decisions on its behalf holds much growth for your soul. (See the chapter called "Big Decisions" in my prior book *Soul Healing with Our Animal Companions* for further help.)

Your animal loves you unconditionally no matter what choices you make about their care. Sometimes part of your soul contract is that you provide them hospice care, and through that experience you learn patience and sacred service to others. There are unlimited potential soul contracts and learnings and of course they are different with every relationship.

If you are in the midst of determining if it is time to lovingly assist your animal back to Spirit, remember this: you will know it in your heart when it is their time.

If possible, know that your beloved animal would appreciate your being with them when their soul releases from their body. There will be situations that unfold where this will not be possible. If the only thing preventing you from being with them is your fear of the emotional pain you will endure, know that you are stronger than you think, and you really do have it within you to be there for them in their final moments. This is a soul-stretching opportunity for your own growth. Lean into the spiritual help around you for support to find the courage needed to continue developing your own inner parenting to release your fears, and ground into the knowing that you will survive this and more.

Creating a sacred ceremony or ritual of your choosing to say goodbye to your beloved companion can help you to process and heal more quickly from the loss. Sometimes it is not an option because of the situation, but even then you can still have a sacred honoring ceremony for them after they're gone, and *they will be there.* The more you can embrace the natural grieving cycles to heal and release *your* pain, the less fear you will have with other animals when a physical challenge arises.

Everything will unfold just as it should. Remember that you have extra angelic and spiritual assistance before, during, and after your animal's passing. Lean into the help that is lovingly provided for you, your animals, and your family. *It is always there. You are never alone.* Honor your animal's soul with gratitude for a life well lived and served, and find solace in knowing that you will see them again. Your love for each other is eternal.

∞ Connecting with Your Animal's Spirit

This technique can be used while your animal companion is still with you, as well as after they have returned to Spirit.

- *Sit comfortably and relax by taking several deep breaths into your heart.*
- *Call upon your animal's soul, and ask them to join you. You can do this telepathically, or by voicing your request out loud, or both. Imagine them sitting in front of you, next to you, or perhaps on your lap.*
- *Continue to breathe directly into your heart. Maybe place a hand on your heart to help you to relax.*
- *Imagine a beautiful metallic golden cord of light connecting your heart to your animal's heart.*
- *Relax and breathe into this sacred heart-to-heart connection. Feel the love flowing through the connection.*
- *In this sacred and loving space, you will be granting them a huge wish if you allow them to send you love and gratitude for all you have done for them.*

🖋 *Breathe and receive.*

🖋 *Share any thoughts with him or her, or ask a question. Express any thoughts you have, no matter the emotion associated with it.*

🖋 *You might sense an answer, see a visual image or certain color, or simply feel their love. Answers to your questions might arrive in that moment, later in a dream, or in a unique way in the days that follow.*

🖋 *Let your animal's soul help you to heal any part of you that is hurting.*

🖋 *Give yourself permission to release and heal. This is a way to honor their soul.*

🖋 *Express gratitude.*

3

The Soul History
of Animals

Do animals accumulate karma too? Do they repeatedly reincarnate to be with the same person? Can you arrange for a specific animal to reincarnate? Can an animal have been another species or even a person in a past life? Do animals have karma to balance with each other? And the most difficult topic of all: Why would an animal choose to be abused?

These questions will be addressed in this enlightening chapter filled with the wisdom of the animal teachers that have graced my life and healing practice for the past two decades. I write about karma and reincarnation in this chapter not through intimate knowledge of the beliefs of Hindus or Buddhists, but through the lens of my personal experiences and healing practice while working with animals and humans to help them clear deep-seated emotional wounds. Your soul history with your animals is a big part of the reason you're repeatedly drawn together. Your shared journeys have likely exceeded more than one lifetime, and your sacred partnership has been paramount to the evolution of both of your souls.

Karma (noun)

According to the tenets of both Hinduism and Buddhism, karma is the sum of a person's actions in this and previous states of existence and as such is viewed as deciding that person's fate in future existences.

Informal: likened to destiny or fate, or that which follows as effect from cause.

When you are aware of and tune in to karma you will notice it playing out in your life, sometimes rather quickly. Have you ever had a car pull out in front in you such that you had to slam on your brakes, then someone pulled out in front of *that* car at the next corner in the same exact manner? The synchronicities of karma are perpetually unfolding in every aspect of life in this way.

Karma can be described as the divine balancer of your conscious and unconscious experiences and the feelings and beliefs birthed from your past choices. Becoming aware of the cause and effect nature of karma provides all beings with an opportunity to intentionally enhance their spiritual DNA through a desire to achieve balance within the self.

When you consciously and intentionally make loving choices, the more profound and long-lasting the transformation is to the blueprint of your soul's underbelly.

From a soul perspective, every person and animal has had experiences that prompt them to choose experiences in this life to balance the scales of their karmic soul. This in turn can proliferate the healing and evolution within everyone the person or animal encounters because of their commitment to consciously make amends. Moving forward, their actions and interactions are intentionally focused on creating positive, good karma, through heartfelt acts filled with unconditional love and kindness.

Animals are wonderful role models and teachers about how to keep the soul in a positive state of karmic balance. They listen without judgment, love unconditionally, and serve others in ways we can only hope to duplicate in this life.

Reincarnation (noun)
    The rebirth of a soul in a new body. A person or animal in whom a particular soul is believed to have been reborn. Informal: a new version of something from the past.

My dear friend Cynthia is a huge dog lover. Cats? Not so much. So I was surprised to learn she had had a childhood cat that she dearly loved. Knowing her aversion to the feline persuasion, I asked Cynthia what it was that she loved about her cat, Molly Ann. Her list was long: Whenever she whistled, Molly Ann would come running to her and always greeted her at the door, ready to engage. Molly Ann would request to go outdoors to do her "business," so Cynthia's family never purchased a litter box. Once outside in the fenced-in backyard, Molly Ann stayed within the confines of the yard . . . not once trying to jump the four-foot fence. She loved playing fetch and learning tricks. She even enjoyed getting a bath!

Molly Ann used to be a dog in a past life. Probably many times.

Early in my spiritual awakening, I read and thoroughly enjoyed the book *Many Lives, Many Masters* by Brian Weiss, M.D. The concept of reincarnation and multiple lives fascinated me because it was something that had never, ever, entered the realm of what I considered possible in the first forty years of my life. Dr. Weiss validated, through his documented past-life regression work, much of what I'd been piecing together in those first few months of my new-to-me, multidimensional life. My preferences in music, home decorations, countries I felt drawn to visit, physical ailments and sensitivities, in addition to phobias and fears, were all tied into my past-life experiences.

Earlier I mentioned that during a period of great loss in my life, I was suddenly able to see into the spirit realm. I would frequently be shown not only memories I had repressed from childhood, but also many of my past lives—the good and the not so good. Because we are here to learn, heal our emotional wounds, and counterbalance our past choices, most of the past lives that came into my awareness were the ones that needed to be rectified. Many of the past lives shown to me were filled with the battles and wars of previous times. It was eye-opening to think my soul could do anything as negative as what I observed it doing in my past lives. During that early stretch of time directly after the lock on my soul's history broke free, I was devastated and ashamed, and I felt powerless to right the actions from my past lives.

The good news is that the more awake and conscious we are right here and right now, the more quickly and easily we can exponentially clear and balance our karma, even if it was created in this very lifetime. And balancing past karmic experiences is not necessarily an eye-for-an-eye situation. Karma can sometimes be cleared, for example, by opening your heart and finding the courage to heal any unworthiness held within yourself, and raising your level of consciousness by serving other beings. Sometimes there is a balancing of a service, like taking care of a being that took care of you during a difficult time in a past life. Most of the time the karma is cleared through an act of kindness that has been pre-arranged to balance the energy between the two beings.

Balancing karma is much faster when the individual who is amending the karma is in a body. And some areas that you desire healing and karmic balancing in can *only* be cleared during a physical incarnation.

 Earth School comes with endless gifts for the courageous ones who lovingly show up for themselves and others.

Another astonishing revelation was realizing that my current animal companions have been with me in previous lives. Toward the end of this chapter I share my soul history with my current cat companions, Bodhi and Rumi. After I'd adopted them, no one was more surprised than I was to recognize their souls. When I realized who one of them had been in his past life, I dropped to my knees in tears to release guilt and pain I had harbored over the six years since I had last seen him. The other cat remains one of my biggest teachers and guides in this life. This book would not have been written without these two light beams coming back to me . . . again!

Through my personal and work experiences, I have also determined that we have a soul group of animals we partner with repeatedly, just like the people in our lives, for mutual evolution and karmic balancing. We have soul groups filled with co-creating companions (two- and four-legged) that we intentionally incarnate with to help each other reach our highest potential. Soul groups are also noted and explained in Michael Newton's book, *Journey of Souls*. There are also other beings, animals, and people that we connect with to simply clear karma and balance the energy exchange between one another. These are two very different types of soul healing contracts.

There are endless reasons an animal might choose to share all or a portion of its life with you. For example, the animals that trigger you negatively might not be from your animal soul group, but perhaps you contracted with them to be a button-pusher to help you to clear unreleased emotions. Or perhaps you were intended to learn compassion and patience from them. On the other end of the spectrum, there might be an animal whose purpose is to remind you of how wonderful you are just when you need it most. Seek to find the higher meaning of their actions and behaviors as this will facilitate an awareness of the gifts your souls planned before you incarnated into the bodies you now inhabit.

Most animal lovers have shared the journey with a couple of animal companions that have made monumental impacts on their soul's growth. It's possible they were your first unconditional love, or supported you through a difficult time, or that their love helped you to heal physically and/or emotionally. You have probably known and loved these animals for many lifetimes. These light beams have their sights set on reminding you of the truth of who you are at your core: a beautiful, loving, worthy, and powerful being.

When a person first meets the animal they are destined to be with, the animal will undoubtedly recognize and choose them. There's a good chance the person will reciprocate the interest, but sometimes they don't recognize the animal's soul until they've spent more time with them. Animals tend to maintain their connection to the Divine more frequently than people do, so their first-class antennae will recall the prebirth agreements and intuitively steer them to connect with the right person(s). It's simply magical. The big picture about how and why the animal and human are attracted to each other is further detailed in chapter 4, "Types of Soul

Contracts Defined," which documents the prebirth planning possibilities between them.

Do animals accumulate karma?

I've concluded that animals can have karmic experiences they seek to balance. Mirroring how people are consciously or unconsciously hoping to equalize their encounters with other beings, animals are also on an evolutionary journey of growth.

When we dearly love a person or an animal, there might be a part of us that wants to take away their pain. Sometimes, this can literally happen. If it wasn't time for the person (or animal) to release that pain back to Spirit for transformation, then it needs to be returned to the point of origin where it was created or there is an imbalance.

Note that if a person or animal *is* ready to release energy because they have received the lesson, made amends, and healed the emotional wound, that's different. That type of clearing can happen naturally, or the energy can release with the assistance of an animal or person, and it simply returns to Spirit. The emotional energy needs to be returned to the other being only when there was an unconscious agenda. For example, the well-meaning person or animal that took the energy of the emotional or physical pain might unconsciously believe it would be easier for them to carry their loved one's pain rather than watch them suffer.

Another way an animal's karma needs to be balanced is if their actions hurt another being physically or emotionally in a past life. If an animal exhibited behaviors and actions that negatively affected another being and they did not balance those feelings while still in that lifetime, they will need to make amends. The animal will likely have an intention to create good karma through sacred service and possibly even serve the specific beings that were affected by their actions. Just as with people, it is possible to balance karma in the same lifetime in which it was created.

While facilitating sessions, I frequently see past lives between the animal and their person as it relates to healing what they have mutually contracted to clear and balance in this life. I will share many of these extraordinary stories in chapter 5, "Tandem Healing Case Studies."

Can you arrange for a specific animal soul to incarnate?
It is possible in certain situations. When you've had an extraordinary connection with one of your animals it's natural to want their soul to return to you. Earth School is not easy, and animals are the safest love that some people will ever experience. It would be wonderful if pets' lives were longer and we got to spend more time with them, especially those souls we have a deep connection with. But they aren't, so the eventual pain of losing an animal is unavoidable.

Many people miss their beloved animal companion so much after they've passed that they intentionally seek help to enable the return of their animal's soul in a different body. I know there are gifted intuitive facilitators who will help you to reunite with your beloved animal in a new animal body.

As part of the research for this book I asked people on several group forums if they'd ever successfully had an animal come back to them with the help of a facilitator. Although no one had, I'm speculating that it has likely proven positive for many people. There *were* quite a few people who stated that they'd achieved their desired outcome by asking for help from a higher power, or simply by talking with the spirit of their departed animal through their heart-to-heart connection.

With the free will all beings have, it is possible to alter the prearranged contracts you have with the animals that you share your heart and home with. If it is in the highest and best interests of your healing and growth, there is an increased chance of success.

Sometimes you desire to reunite with the same animal because you are still grieving their loss and there is unreleased emotional pain. There are many healthy ways to release your grief and in turn nurture yourself and begin to heal any preexisting patterns of looking outside yourself to fill your need to feel loved. A few examples are grief loss counseling, daily meditation, exercise, and energy therapy. If a person represses their grief and emotional pain over the long term, they will have more fear around losing any animal and might even decide not to share their lives with animals anymore as it is too painful when they pass.

If you are someone who represses your grief and believes in reincarnation, then arranging for your animal to come back to you might appear to be a logical answer to alleviate your pain. However, this is a temporary solution since you will probably outlive them again. If you continue to repress your past grief and pain, it will show up as a physical ailment, either in yourself or possibly in your animal (if they have returned to you). In addition, you may inadvertently contribute to creating an ongoing, underlying fear of losing them again.

My Recommendation: The animals that grace your life are all part of a divinely orchestrated plan that *you* co-created. Begin to trust the timing that you and your animal companions have carefully selected for your mutual growth. Your Higher Selves are acutely aware of what you both want to accomplish while in Earth School. It is a potential growth opportunity for you to surrender into the wisdom at your core and trust the higher plan. The right and perfect animal(s) *will* show up at the right and perfect time.

Think of the animals yet to come into your life as gifts you are blessed to unwrap while you discover together what you both hoped to feel, heal, and learn by sharing your journey.

Can animal souls have been another animal species, or a person, in a past life?

The answer is unequivocally yes! The odds are very high that one of your animals has probably shared its life with you previously as another species. Perhaps you've even identified what type of animal it was in a previous life.

Days after adopting my kitten MaiTai and bringing him home, I was flabbergasted when I noticed he was sitting up like a dog in a "begging" stance and repeatedly swinging his front paws together. He did this all his life whenever he wanted something. I knew that, in his first few months of life, he hadn't had a secret kitten trainer who taught dog tricks to cats. The behavior was wired into his soul's DNA. How could that happen, unless he was a dog in a previous life? MaiTai was always doglike. He loved playing fetch (he retrieved the toy and dropped it in front of me), was incentivized by food, and even enjoyed walking on a leash with a cat halter.

I've repeatedly heard similar reports from clients. "My dog is more like a cat." Or "My horse acts like a dog." Although most of the time when I observe an animal client's past life, it was the same species, sometimes during a healing session it comes into my awareness that an animal was a different species in a past life. Cats and dogs more frequently share their lives with people. Interacting with and serving people can expedite their soul's growth due to the complexity and depth of the interactions. Animal lovers will agree that they have been transformed for the better and healed faster because of the unwavering service of animals.

Animals can choose to be another species if they so desire for growth or simply to have the experience. On occasion I've seen animals with the soul of a person who chose to incarnate into an animal to be with that person. This soul can be a spirit guide from the person's soul group or even a past relative. These incarnations are designed to help the person open their heart, heal, and grow more quickly. The person having the human experience senses the familiarity and safety of unconditional love offered from the animal and leans into its healing gifts.

Do animals have karma to balance with each other?
Animals *can* have karma to amend with another animal. You'll know if something karmic has happened between your fur babies because there is an immediate disdain when the animals "recognize" each other's soul. The new animal brought into the home might even be returned or rehomed after a volatile reaction to, or from, a pet already in the home. The good news is that it's very feasible that this initial brief interaction between them balanced their karma.

There are a lot of ways to interpret the interaction of animals seeking to balance their karmic experiences. It's possible for karma to be quickly cleared between two animals. Perhaps the animals' roles are reversed this time around. Think of an unleashed dog running up to another dog with intent to do it harm. Perhaps in a future life, the roles are reversed just enough for the karma to clear—and a simple growl or release of energy and consciousness is enough to make that happen. When this occurs, there's no need for them to become best friends and live happily ever after once the karma has been corrected.

There is always a higher plan between two animals with karma to balance and endless potential ways to implement it. As best you can in what can be a difficult situation where safety should always come first, know that your actions are typically also part of their higher soul plan. Have compassion with yourself when making tough choices and decisions in these cases. Connect to them heart-to-heart and ask for signs for the right and perfect next step to make. Trust your connection with them to guide you.

Buddy & Sugar

Debbie's father had recently passed, which left her dad's dog, Buddy, needing a new home. Debbie decided to adopt Buddy even though her husband, Joe, wasn't excited about the idea of bringing another pet into their house. She contacted me to arrange a healing session for Buddy to help him release his grief and to assist him with transitioning from a situation where he was the only animal in the house to being in a new home that already had two dogs and two cats.

As soon as I connected with Buddy, I was shown that he had unresolved karma with one of Debbie's other dogs, Sugar. I could feel their angst toward each other. I gave Debbie a softened heads-up that there might be a little karma between the two that needed balancing. I suggested that she telepathically send Sugar and Buddy visuals of them getting along and that they be slowly introduced.

From the moment Buddy and Sugar saw each other, they didn't like each other. At all. But here's where the story gets interesting. Buddy, seeking a safe place in the house away from Sugar, would glue himself to Joe, who frequently worked in his home office.

The following year, Debbie and Joe decided to go their separate ways and get a divorce. The only animal that went with Joe was Buddy because they had become inseparable. There was a higher plan and reason all along for Buddy to be with Joe. Sugar and Buddy never became friends, and there weren't any actual physical fights between them, but they probably cleared their karma with one another. Sugar was the stronger personality, but perhaps it was the opposite in their last life together.

Another level of this story has to do with the relationship between Debbie and Joe. Frequently I see two animals in the house reflecting the human couple's relationship. The animals might be mirroring the two humans' outward interaction or their unspoken thoughts and emotions.

Why would an animal *choose* to be abused?

This must be *the* most difficult subject for animal lovers. Yet I feel it is an important topic to broach due to its potential to raise your awareness through learning about some of the reasons animals might choose, at a soul level, to experience physical abuse. This subject arrives with a lot of emotional triggers and is actually very complex in nature. My intention is to shine some light on it to give you some food for thought—and hopefully, a little comfort as well.

Many animal lovers avoid looking at or listening to anything related to animal abuse. Other times people find themselves filled with anger about how animals are treated and have even lost hope in humanity when they hear stories about some people's unconscionable and cruel actions.

In general, animal lovers tend to be empathetic. Having empathy is a gift. Think of someone you know that (unfortunately) doesn't have empathy. Which way would you prefer to be? Having empathy for others and relating to what another being is going through is the foundation of emotional maturity.

Empathetic people can tend to gravitate to animals instead of people. Animals are safe to love, and they mirror the ability to feel the emotions of others and their surroundings. Animals maintain and nurture their connection to a higher power, and this draws people to them like magnets. People are inherently attracted to those who lift them up and provide a judgment-free zone. Animals are masters at providing people with an environment where they feel safe to be themselves.

Being empathetic can create an elevated emotional reaction upon hearing about an animal's suffering. The thought of any animal being abused can sicken the stomach of an animal lover. I know it turns my stomach.

If you have ever been abused, mistreated, or oppressed by a person, your emotional reaction to animal abuse is amplified because on some level you are literally relating to the animal. This can further serve to reiterate an unconscious belief that people are not safe. Our soul is wired with the memory of every experience we've ever had, the kind and the not so kind. Ultimately, this is the lens through which we can relate to others and feel empathy or mercy toward them, or not.

In the first eight years of my life, I experienced much abuse. All types . . . physical, emotional, and sexual. I also watched animals being abused and sometimes even losing their life by the same men who hurt me. When the memories of those experiences were unlocked, I was writhing in pain, anger, and shame. But after undergoing several years of a deep inner healing journey, I began to realize that my soul had orchestrated it all to balance my karma and learn many valuable lessons. This brought me so much peace. Knowing the bigger picture and purpose behind my soul's choices alleviated an old victim pattern.

My early experiences induced in me lifelong feelings of empathy, acceptance, and compassion toward others. I experienced this because I had been shown none of those qualities by my abusers. Abuse can be mirrored, replicated, or used to catapult you forward by showing you how you never want to treat another being. It may bestow upon you the desire to do the opposite of your abuser by fostering empathy and an inner yearning to treat others with loving kindness. The first two options—mirroring and replicating—are less likely to bring the long-term results you might prefer, but be kind to yourself as you unlearn what you were modeled and shown. There is always more time for every soul lesson to ignite a new level of awareness within you. Every being has prearranged their life experiences to help them to *feel* their way to the more conscious emotions. There are endless options and ways to reach and integrate your soul's desired outcome.

Amazingly, many animals continue to feel and express compassion even in the midst of being abused. The good news is that most abused animals rapidly heal in a loving environment. Animals are wired to instinctively, and sometimes literally, *shake it off,* and as a result, they don't keep reliving their past abuse. Some are haunted longer than others by their negative experiences, but that might also be by choice. In such cases, perhaps they contracted with a person to heal their mirrored emotional wounds simultaneously or the agreement was to allow the person's soul to grow by learning patience by taking care of the scared animal.

Sometimes an animal's abuse story gets shared over and over again. My sense from working with previously abused animals is that they would prefer that the people in their lives focus on the present moment. Sharing an animal's abuse story will instantaneously lower the vibration in a room. They are masters at living in the present moment and would prefer that you focus on the positive new chapter in their lives. They are thankful for your help and ready to move forward.

Here are some of the reasons an animal's soul plan might include experiencing physical abuse:

- They are balancing the karmic experiences of their previous lives by seeking to enhance their levels of compassion, love, or empathy (perhaps by feeling the opposite of these very qualities).

- An animal might willingly choose to incarnate with high hope that through a consistent expression of love and compassion toward their abuser, the person will have a breakthrough to feel empathy and remorse. Or perhaps the animal helps the person to begin to know and feel a glimmer of love for quite possibly the first time. These animals are sometimes very old souls that are serving at a very high level to bring light into the darkest of hearts.

- Sometimes the animal soul willingly chooses to incarnate into an animal's body to advocate, through their actions, for animal rights or the enactment of laws to protect the environment. They might choose to be an animal that's been involved in an oil spill, or a fighting ring, or maybe a zoo that's not treating its animals well, all with the hope that the abuse will motivate people to take action that will in turn help innumerable other animals.

- An animal might choose to endure a person's abuse or live in captivity because they're serving a larger population of people. Perhaps it's a situation where the public can learn more about their species and bring joy to those who watch them perform.

There are endless experiences that animals can choose to serve humanity and other animals in order to evolve their souls. After any animal has endured physical abuse, I try to imagine them being welcomed back to Spirit and given the animal equivalent of the Nobel Peace Prize.

Another gift you can give them is to utilize the moment that you are emotionally triggered to release your emotions. When you see or hear about an animal being abused, and suddenly feel emotions such as grief, anger, fear, and emotional pain, always utilize the opportunity to release these emotions in healthy ways. The release will help you feel better, *and* the animal has been able to add to his or her good karma pool by helping you lighten your load.

 Animals are counting on people to act on their behalf to create a kinder world for all beings.

Courage (noun)
    The ability to do something that frightens one. For example, "She called on all her courage to face the ordeal." Informal: strength in the face of pain or grief.

Your animals are on an evolutionary journey too. Honor their courage and how they've shown up to serve humanity.

Know that they chose to have courageous soul experiences to evolve and balance the scales of their karma. When you hear about an animal abuse situation, reach for the higher purpose. Heal anything within you that gets triggered. Then take positive action to help in the way or ways that you can. Sometimes that means prayer, donations, healing, calling your congressperson, writing grants, or recruiting additional help to change a law or situation. Honor the animal that has chosen the more difficult and courageous road for its soul growth.

All people and animals that have chosen to incarnate on our beautiful planet are born having enough courage within to respectfully help others. Walking through your fears to help another being immeasurably helps you both.

I hope and pray for a time when neither animals nor humans suffer any type of abuse. Until then, we must do what we can to make the world a kinder place for all its inhabitants. One of the best ways to begin is by embracing an inner healing journey and healing your past wounds. Then you will be brighter, lighter, and better able to enhance the lives of others.

My Soul History with Bodhi and Rumi

After my beloved senior cats MaiTai and Sundance passed within months of each other, I declared to my closest friends and family that I wasn't going to adopt another animal for a while. MaiTai and Sundance had both been in hospice-type care situations for a year or two, and I needed time to grieve and heal. I had a book tour and plenty of traveling on my schedule with the release of *Soul Healing with Our Animal Companions*. Even though it was the first time in thirty-five years that I didn't have an animal companion, I decided it wasn't a good time to bring new furkids into the house. Everyone understood. It made sense. I'd take a break. Maybe a long one.

Yeah . . . sure. That was my 3-D plan anyway.

The visions started coming to me in meditation. They were always the same: six gray kittens playing together. I was also seeing the number 222 several times each day. I'm in contact weekly with a handful of no-kill animal shelters because I donate healing sessions to them as part of my service work. Therefore I'm exposed to many animals that are seeking adoption. *Somehow,* I found out that two of the rescue organizations each had a litter of six gray kittens.

During my workshops and with clients, I frequently share the importance of following one's guidance. This includes God-winks and nudges, however they may arrive on your doorstep. Even with my obvious resistance, I was aware of the relevance and importance of moving forward to determine if there were two kittens in either of these two litters, preferably a bonded pair, that were meant to be with me. If things didn't come together easily, I'd know it wasn't meant to be yet.

My heart was racing when I walked into the kitten room at Good Mews Animal Foundation. I invited the souls of my beloved MaiTai and Sundance to guide me during this important meet and greet.

When I adopt an animal, I ask them for obvious signs so it'll be clear that they're the one for me. When I'd first met Sundance eighteen years ago, I was indecisive, even though she was the only kitten in her litter that hung out on my lap numerous times. So I left the room to clear my head and ask for clarity.

Upon returning, she was asleep in my purse.

The morning of my visit at Good Mews I decided I would sit on the floor in the center of their free-roaming kitten room and simply wait to see if I was chosen by a bonded pair. There were at least a dozen kittens running around, all of varying coloring, fur length, and ages. As soon as I sat down, one of the gray kittens walked over and sat on my lap. He was constantly watching one of his brothers and would occasionally leave to chase and play with him but always returned to my lap. After a little while his brother decided to join us. The three of us then had a wonderful time getting acquainted.

Not one other kitten showed any interest. I had already decided to move forward with the adoption of the two kittens when one of their volunteers shared that they knew their birth date, which is rare for rescue groups. It was February 22 . . . as in . . . 2.22.

The following week my new teachers and companions, Bodhi and Rumi, moved in with me. And then things got *really* interesting.

Here are their soul stories.

Rumi's Astonishing Surprise

After an adjustment period of a month or so, the kittens' personalities began revealing themselves. While all animals have personality traits specific to their species, each one has its own unique personality, as you know, with certain qualities and habits.

Rumi has an adorable, fun-loving, surfer-dude personality. Easygoing. He loves life. He embodies joy. He appreciates and plays with every toy. Has a major hair fetish. Water lover. Toilet paper connoisseur. Window blind rattler.

Rumi fearlessly runs *toward* the sound of the vacuum and hair dryer and wants to play with them. When he craves one-on-one "mommy time," he repeatedly jumps on my lap affectionately and is so excited that he falls off and then instantly jumps back up. I call it "wiggle-worm time" with this sweet indigo kitty. Rumi would never apply for the alpha cat gig as that would be way too much responsibility and not as much fun.

When we lock eyes, he receives the requests that I send him telepathically and instantly responds. He is sensitive and can be a sponge for my emotions. Physically, Rumi has many food sensitivities, which consistently show up in his colon.

Our journey took an unexpected shift when I gave Rumi his first energy healing session. As soon as we connected heart-to-heart, he surprised me with a heart-fusion soul greeting. For five amazing and euphoric minutes, our souls were fused at the heart within a sphere of golden white light of the highest vibration imaginable. It circled through us, and as it did, I immediately recognized his soul as we shared unconditional love and gratitude. There were tears of joy running down my face. I recall whispering out loud, "It's you," as the memories of our prior lives together and love for each other came flooding into my awareness.

I saw Rumi's most recent life with me as a barn cat I'd named Blossom about twelve years prior.

Blossom

It wasn't surprising to discover there was cat living in the loft of the barn behind the home I was renting. We animal lovers are magnets for strays. Soon thereafter I noticed two small kittens running behind Matilda, the resident barn cat. As soon as it was appropriate to do so, I got the mom and kittens neutered. The three of them always had plenty of food and even comfy beds. Blossom, named before I knew his gender, was the only cat of the three that desired a connection with me. Outside, he followed me around everywhere, and we were good buds. He was a hoot and was always up for playing and being loved on.

I always had a strong sense that Blossom and I knew each other. He reminded me of my first cat, Khalua. Khalua was one of the, if not *the,* greatest animal teachers of my life. She was my first unconditional love. She was the first spirit I saw and interacted with on the other side. Khalua was an adorable calico cat that I'd lost to colon cancer weeks after my mother passed. I dedicated my first book to her, for her teachings had brought unparalleled positive transformation to my life.

When Blossom was two years old, I bought a house and was preparing to move. I didn't want to leave him and was very torn. My indoor cats, Sundance and MaiTai, had very vocal objections to him. A wonderful neighbor was going to continue feeding the feline family in the barn after I left. I tried to get a sense from Blossom about what he wanted me to do. In the past I'd always received clear messages from him, but this situation felt like a conundrum.

Weeks before I moved, a neighbor came over one afternoon to share that an hour earlier, Blossom had darted out of the tall brush that lined the dirt road between our properties, directly in front of his son's car. He died on impact and did not suffer. I was heartbroken and knew the timing was no coincidence.

Rumi

Rumi shared, during the merging of our hearts and soul memories, that he'd wanted to experience being my outdoor companion as Blossom. He was happy with that life and had intentionally chosen to leave quickly.

It was astonishing to learn, through my heart connection with Rumi, that his was the same soul as Blossom *and* Khalua. Khalua had lived as my indoor cat for twelve years. Suddenly, I remembered her as if it were yesterday and knew that Khalua and Rumi's soul were one and the same. Khalua had the same surfer-dude personality and the same exact qualities that Rumi had—even the colon issues. And they all three had the exact same look in their eyes that I recognized as belonging to the same soul.

While I have believed since my awakening that our animals reincarnate with us, this was truly remarkable to personally experience. I hope to further embrace Rumi's go-with-the-flow mind-set, as well as his belief that each and every moment is a gift to enjoy.

I find myself wondering what additional life teachings Rumi has in store for me and how our lives will unfold this time around with my new awareness of our soul history. It will be different, because I'm different. Rumi is more confident and independent than Khalua was, which reflects the changes in me since we last shared a home. This was yet another validation that when we heal *our* inner wounds and begin to serve others, all beings we love will benefit.

Finding Peace with My Humanity—Bodhi's Gift

Bodhi's story is more difficult to write. Our relationship beautifully represents this chapter's intention to learn about our soul partnerships with animals and the higher purpose within each alliance. So I'm diving into a pool of courage held within me and sharing the vulnerability of my humanity as I bear witness to how each one of us is growing through our experiences.

Sassafras

In the fall of 2012, a feral mama cat and her litter of kittens showed up in my backyard. Colder nights would soon follow, given that winter was coming. I decided to help the family and hoped to find them loving homes. I enlisted the help and advice of two friends involved with rescue organizations, both of whom were very experienced in the rescue of feral cats. Soon I had four kittens in a room, all of which were approximately eight to ten weeks old.

Sassafras was sweet and bold and knew what he wanted (which was usually climbing up my body and "claiming" me). He had more fear than the others, but once he trusted me, he was all in. He had an alpha personality and would hiss and growl at the other kittens during mealtime, worried he might not get enough, and in true hunter mentality, he was protective of toys after he'd "captured" them.

Once the kittens had healed from a bout of upper respiratory tract infections and were healthy and comfortable with people, I began seeking homes for them. When my social networking skills didn't yield any possibilities, I began taking applications using a form I received from my friend's animal shelter organization. With advice from my rescue buddies, I decided that a price tag of seventy-five dollars per kitten would aid in diverting people with negative intentions. (Working with rescue organizations, I am frequently exposed to the unthinkable things that can happen to animals that are given away for free.)

A nice lady called about adopting Sassafras and wanted to meet him. The application looked great, and their interaction was good. I was thrilled. She paid the money, and I put him in the carrier, and we said our goodbyes.

Later that evening, I began to have a nagging feeling about the woman and wondered if I'd checked her out enough. When you spend so much time fostering and caring for these little ones, you love them and want to protect them forever. All that night I replayed every conversation in my head. I wasn't sure if it was simply unfounded fears or intuition that was behind my worries. I decided to call her in the morning to check on him.

The phone number no longer worked. I googled the woman's name and couldn't find anything online, let alone a photo of the woman I'd met. I began to panic and assume the worse. I finally decided to drive to the address given on the application, even though I was uncertain what I would do when I got there. It turned out that it wasn't a real address. I had no way to ever find this woman and recover Sassafras.

I was beside myself with frustration and filled with agony. I had many, many sleepless nights thinking about what Sassafras might have been enduring or was currently enduring. It filled my thoughts, and I turned my anger inward. The energy healer I go to regularly softly pointed out that I was relating to what I *imagined* he was going through and suggested detaching for my own well-being. In positive moments I would send his soul love and see him surrounded with light. This exercise was beneficial for me and I hope for Sassafras as well.

Thank goodness the three other kittens were adopted by very loving homes. In that first year, I received updates and photos of them that warmed my heart. But I couldn't forget Sassafras and my remorse about letting him go. I never had a good feeling about the whole thing and what he may have experienced.

Over the years I thought about it less and intentionally tried to pivot my thought process when my thoughts would begin swirling about what might have happened to him. However, I was never able to forgive myself.

Bodhi

There was no doubt about it, Bodhi had a lot more fear of people and life in general than Rumi did. My vet diagnosed him with what was (probably) kitty herpes, which showed up for Bodhi as symptoms of sneezing and watery eyes. It is stress reactive.

This did not slow him down, though, as he was, and still is, lightning fast and has a level of athleticism to behold. It is beautiful to watch the ease and grace with which he jumps from the floor to the top of the refrigerator or goes after a toy. I nicknamed him Cheetah Man. He has the focus of an incredible hunter. While he is comfortable in his independence, he is very loyal and kind. It is easy to see his light and his desire to heal, trust, and love more intimately.

Soon after the kitten brothers moved in with me, I noticed Bodhi's food aggression with his brother, as well as his hissing and protection of his favorite toys. He is the alpha cat. I began facilitating healing sessions with the hope of helping him release his fears and heal his body since nothing else was shifting his physical symptoms. Those first few sessions with Bodhi were very intense. There was endless releasing of lower vibrational fear-based soul memories and the emotions birthed from those experiences. They were from past lives where people and other animals around him were unempathetic and abusive.

During his first session, I knew, based on the visuals he showed me of his most recent past life, in addition to their having the same personalities, that Bodhi was the same soul as Sassafras. Never had I been happier and more relieved to know that I now had a chance to help this beautiful soul heal from his past. I assumed that my Higher Self had asked him to come back to me to clear my karma and make amends so that I could finally forgive myself for having let Sassafras go.

The release in my heart was palpable as I made a commitment to aid in healing his emotional wounds. I literally dropped to my knees and began releasing tears of gratitude for this wonderful opportunity, amazed at how our souls had reconnected for the benefit of us both.

Bodhi responded very well to the sessions, and his physical symptoms completely disappeared. He is such a dear, and in getting to know his personality more, I realize how much we are alike. We share an inner strength and a caution with people. There are also parallels of our past abuse *and* how, despite everything, we move forward and focus courageously on our goals.

Since Bodhi's initial healing sessions, there have only been a couple of times I've heard him hiss at Rumi. He is beginning to know, as I am at a new level, that there will always be *enough* to fulfill our needs.

Bodhi and Rumi

How fortunate I am to have a mirror in front of me with which to gauge my personal progress. When I look into Bodhi's eyes, I see a beautiful soul that is powerful beyond measure. He will be fine. Heck, he *is* fine. He's amazing, and I'm fortunate to have his teachings in my life.

Interestingly, just last week I was sharing Bodhi's story with my friend Tony. He asked me how my book was progressing. With my awareness of his Buddhist beliefs in karma and reincarnation, I decided to tell Tony the story of Sassafras coming back as Bodhi and how fortunate I was to have the chance to clear my karma with him.

Tony touched my hand and gave me half a smile and said, "Do you really think that's how karma works?" He gently continued, "You were trying to help the kitten by taking him in and trying to find him a home. You did not intentionally harm him in any way. You actually created good karma through your actions."

All I could do was sit there looking at him because I'd heard the truth and simplicity of his words. They went straight to my heart for yet another much needed level of peace and healing and insight to take place. Spirit spoke through him with the words I needed to hear to shift my thinking.

I would easily have seen the same level of truth and wisdom with one of my clients in a similar situation. Apparently, I get to be human too. It was finally time to be compassionate and kind with *myself* about the fact that I had allowed Sassafras to be adopted by someone who proved to have ulterior motives. There was a higher soul purpose to the entire situation that was just beginning to reveal itself to me.

Bodhi and Rumi have already changed me for the better and now I get to share their teachings to help others know that there is always more to the story than meets the eye. I think, perhaps, that this book is also part of *their* souls' purpose. And the best thing is that I have the honor and joy of sharing this conscious journey with two loving and kind brothers that will continue to show me more about myself and how to enjoy being in this present moment.

SACRED INSIGHTS

Your soul history with your animals has created a finely tuned plan that you are living out with them today. Both of you are aspiring to balance your karma, heal, grow, and joyfully evolve together. Every experience you share has a higher purpose. Reaching for the gifts and higher perspective will help you feel better more quickly—especially when in the middle of a difficult experience with your animal companion.

Empower your awareness of karma and reincarnation so that it's a catalyst to help you make conscious decisions from a place of compassion and kindness in all your interactions, especially with yourself. Try as best you can to release fear-based emotions in healthy ways instead of onto other beings or by beating yourself up. In the midst of having a "human moment," the best thing you can do is clear your mind, breathe into your heart, lean into your spiritual connection, find compassion with yourself, and integrate the gifts of the experience as best you can.

This one life is precious and important in the grand scheme of your soul's pilgrimage. If your soul has aggressively chosen to balance a lot of past experiences this go-around, in other words, have a lot of difficult experiences, you might want to team up with a practitioner to engage in a deep inner healing journey. At the minimum, I highly recommend being proactive in tending to your spiritual connection to a higher power. In addition, intend to work on your "inner observer muscle" so you can more easily view situations from a higher perspective.

Find comfort in knowing that you and your animals
will survive everything, and your hearts will forever
be connected.

Give yourself a heaping dose of gratitude and compassion for being so courageous and brave to do the healing work you have chosen to do in this life with your animal(s). Know that when you begin to love yourself as much as they love you, everyone benefits. Love is liberating!

You are the powerful creator of all you
experience, both the challenges you planned
before you were born and the healing you create
in this and in each "now" moment.

ROBERT SCHWARTZ

4

Types of Soul Contracts Defined

A HIGHER PERSPECTIVE

Since my awakening and embracing my new life path, I have been intrigued and fascinated by the higher purpose of our soul's evolutionary journey. I feel compelled and driven to reach for the higher perspective within the day-to-day experiences, especially those that elicit fear-based reactions such as anger, shame, frustration, judgment, jealousy, or insecurity. When we realize that every experience in our lives is always unfolding for our highest good, we feel less stressed about the future.

Seeking the gifts and higher perspective within each experience has the ability to soothe and console us in the midst of difficult times. When you take a step back and observe a situation from a detached viewpoint, it diffuses the fear-based thoughts and sheds light on the part within you that is being triggered. Then you are more apt to react from a grounded and more aware place versus through the lens of unhealed emotional wounds. Triggers are simply indications that it's a perfect time to pause, reflect, and look within to determine what is at the root of your reaction, which has shown up for you to see more clearly.

You can apply this same principle to your animal companions by reaching for the higher purpose in their actions, behaviors, and physical issues. Then you can more easily interpret your animal's experiences *and* your emotional response to them. Think of it as sprinkling a little stardust on the situation, and voila! You suddenly see a different form of communication coming from your animal that wasn't even on the radar to begin with.

I remember when a friend traveled to Antarctica with the anticipated highlight of being able to see the penguins. She and the other hundred or so other passengers on the boat had finally arrived at their destination. The captain excitedly waved an arm and professed, "There they are!" The passengers looked and looked but didn't see any penguins. Then all of a sudden, their eyes focused differently and directly in front of them were thousands of penguins!

This is a great example of what transpires when you change your focus and perceive a situation, person, animal, or experience from a new level. By intentionally shifting your focus you become aware of a new perspective. Sometimes all it takes is a new vantage point to shift your outlook.

Growth happens when you are open to changing your mind through seeking the higher perspective and then allow a transformative shift in consciousness to unfold.

Part of my mission is to provide a fresh new perspective on how people can choose to interact with their animals. When an animal lover recognizes and leans into the higher purpose of their soul agreements with their animals, and the reason they are together, the relationship takes on new meaning.

DEFINING A SOUL CONTRACT

A soul contract is an agreement between two beings to expand their growth in this lifetime. Before your animals incarnated to be with you, your Higher Selves agreed upon the lessons and growth needed for your mutual healing and development. For ease in understanding this material I interchangeably use the words *agreement* and *contract*.

Through my work over the last two decades I've identified and documented seven types of soul agreements. Indeed there are seven different conceptual approaches that animals and humans use to engage in intentional soul communication for their mutual growth. Held within each level are distinctive ways that you are helping each other to live out your preplanned agreements.

Agreements can be with any animal that has touched you in ways small and large. This can include the animals that you live with but will also be animals that have briefly been in your life, in addition to animals in nature.

The types of soul contracts are diverse, and all are important to your growth and to your animal's growth. Since being in a body comes with challenges, the prearranged contracts can fluctuate and change as unexpected experiences potentially thwart the original soul plan. Challenges are created to learn specific lessons necessary to ignite the richness and depth of the positive emotions you and your animals desire to feel.

All beings have free will, and life is known to bring a few curveballs. Although it's rare for a soul plan to veer off course, if your experiences have caused your inner soul Siri to recalculate the route, it is possible to manifest a similar or even improved outcome for your soul progression. Your light team and animal companions are aligned in such a way to help keep you on the path you designed. This takes the form of synchronicities, gentle nudges via your thoughts, and inspirational ideas and actions.

There is an unlimited amount of time to evolve and learn. Every being aspires to feel more peace, joy, and unconditional love more often, and each being's path and timing is unique. Animals and humans will instinctively set the right and perfect tempo and timing for their Earth lessons.

The closer you become emotionally to your animals, the more engaged they are in your soul's growth. And in turn you will both agree to implement contracts for your mutual growth. If you are an introvert or empath it is more likely that your soul has turned to animals to collaborate with in order to facilitate your personal transformation.

As you read through the following contract types, notice which agreements you can relate to with your current or past animal companion(s). There are usually many types of agreements operating in each of your animal collaborations. Every agreement, at its core, is rooted in unconditional love for the other being and is agreed upon in advance by both beings in the relationship. When there are multiple people in the house in relationship with the animal, each pairing has their own personalized agreement. That's why two people will describe or see different traits in the same animal and respond differently to their behaviors.

The contracts are designed to assist both the animal and their human to heal and enrich their soul development on the path to feeling more love and less suffering.

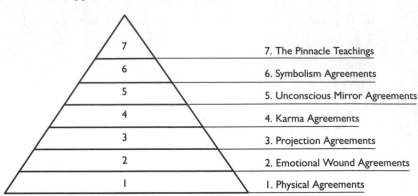

The Animal-Human Soul Contract Types

LEVEL ONE: PHYSICAL AGREEMENTS

Have you ever had an animal companion that just "happened" to have the same physical issue you do? Bad hip? Diabetes? Allergies? This is more common than you might think. When I was a young adult in my twenties and thirties, my animals frequently manifested my same exact physical issues. Before I embarked on an inner healing journey, I had a plethora of physical ailments, and my cats were always ill—with *my* stuff. When my cat Vasi developed asthma a month after my diagnosis of asthma I was astounded. It was no coincidence!

Animals can and will mirror or carry their person's physical issues or they may do both. Typically, it's rooted in energy transference originating from a deep love and desire to serve the other being by taking away their pain. However, the animal's soul also has past and current life experiences that will manifest similar issues as their person due to the undeniable force of *like attracts like*. Like beings are magnetized toward each other, and this level of agreement frequently unfolds in very bonded animal-human pairings.

Another slightly different agreement on this physical level is the fact that an animal can absorb the energy from an area of the person's body where there is a surplus of energetic/emotional congestion, yet it hasn't developed physically (in the person). Frequently during animal sessions, I'll detect energetic congestion in a particular area of their body, and the person shares afterward that the animal has no physical issues there, but they themselves do.

Let's walk through an example. If a person has a tendency to hold back on expressing themselves, they might have repressed emotions held energetically at the throat and jaw. Their animal companion might lovingly agree to absorb and carry that energy through sacred service to their beloved person. If the person continues to struggle to express themselves and speak from their heart, the energy the animal is carrying for their person could manifest into a physical ailment. Keeping with this example, the animal might then develop tracheal, dental, or esophageal issues.

Your animal intentionally and lovingly agrees, at a soul level, to absorb your physical energy. Their actions simultaneously serve as a mirror of motivation for their person to heal their past emotional wounds. Animals would never want you to feel guilty about anything they are carrying on your behalf. They lovingly signed up for this agreement. And yet they are still aware that their human, at a soul level, is also hoping they will spot the reflection's higher purpose to induce healing in the right and perfect timing.

It's a beautiful unfolding of events when someone realizes that their animal's physical ailment is a divinely orchestrated message just for them. And I've witnessed the magic of an animal's miraculous healing that sometimes arrives soon after the person begins working on healing the emotional wound that is causing the physical manifestation.

When you are going through an especially difficult time your animals might exhibit more of a physical reaction to your energy and emotions. Amazingly they are trying to help you to release some of your emotions. Practicing good self-care is the best way to help you and your animals while you are going through a challenging and stressful time. They are much more likely to absorb and mirror back to you what you are repressing, rather than what you are beautifully releasing in healthy ways such as crying, exercising, and meditating.

Different breeds of animals tend to have physical issues that are more predictable, but those experiences are also chosen in advance. Everything lines up in miraculous ways by your Higher Selves as you agree to work on these things together. With this level of agreement, the weak physical areas of your body are likely to be their weak physical areas as well. Humans can also absorb their animal's energy, which can manifest into physical issues too. However, this is not nearly as common as the animal carrying their person's physical issue.

One of the keys to helping your animals feel better is to amp up your self-love. When you are giving yourself the love and care *you* need and deserve, this dramatically increases the vibration in the heart and soul of both you and your animal. When my many physical ailments all began to *magically* go away due to my intentional focus to heal my emotional wounds with energy healing sessions, my animals suddenly got healthier too.

LEVEL TWO: EMOTIONAL
WOUND AGREEMENTS

These soul agreements are active in almost every animal-human relationship. When this is realized and fully understood, these soul contracts set in motion the potential for life-changing, positive differences in animals and their humans. The mirrors of truth in these agreements are undeniable.

As I documented in my first book, *Soul Healing with Our Animal Companions,* early into my work with animals I was astonished to discover that animals hold the same energetic wound protection patterns that the humans in their life do. There are literally energetic patterns of protection that people and animals unconsciously create to keep an unhealed emotional wound concealed until the psyche has grown and healed enough to release it. The emotional wounding that sets up shop in the body needs to be cleared before the physical symptoms can permanently heal. Often the original emotional wound can be traced back to early childhood, the womb, and most probably a past life, but the psyche brilliantly represses the wound and protects the person or animal until they have created the internal emotional maturity to endure the release of the initial emotional pain.

The five core emotional wounds are abandonment, betrayal, terror, invasiveness, and detachment from the core self. Almost every manner of negative behavior from your animal originates from an unhealed emotional wound within themselves *or* within you. As a result, your animal might be exhibiting behaviors such as aggression, overprotecting their person or the house or yard, constant licking, overeating, incessant barking, or inappropriate elimination.

People and animals will mirror the same emotional wounds and energetic patterns of protection. Within this level of contracts, there is an agreed upon team effort to heal these wounds *together* through their strong reflection. When people begin to actively heal their emotional wounds, the animal mirroring their emotional wounds will similarly benefit, allowing them to automatically heal with the shift of energy in their person.

If the animal lover is unaware of this agreement dynamic, typically their focus is solely on helping the animal heal their physical and behavioral issues. When a person realizes their animal is mirroring their unhealed emotional wound, it can bring much light to the center of their *shared* wounds. Many times I've seen people proactively begin a deep inner healing journey, only to find that their animals have raised their vibration too, which mirrors their human's new level of wellness. Animals will then exhibit fewer physical issues and/or negative behaviors.

It might be difficult for some people to give themselves much needed self-care due to having unconscious resistance, guilt (engrained selflessness), or fear. Having the skill set required to provide good internal parenting is a muscle each person must create to effectively heal their emotional wounds. Embarking on an inner healing journey is actually a form of self-love and will help the animals too. Healing alongside your animal is the ultimate goal of Emotional Wound Agreements.

Mary & Molly

For many months, to no avail, Mary read through hundreds of petfinder.com dog profiles searching for the right and perfect dog to be a companion for her other dog, Winston. She immediately fell in love the moment she read Molly's write-up and instinctively *knew* Molly was "the one." Molly had been abused and neglected as a backyard breeder's dog prior to getting to the rescue organization. She is a sensitive soul and has continuously expressed some anxiety and fear. She has always been a bit standoffish and needs her space to feel safe. Sometimes she shakes visibly. These behaviors and traits point toward an unhealed invasiveness wound, one of the five types of emotional wounds.

Molly and Winston got along well, and she seemed calmer when Winston was around. Unfortunately, Winston transitioned four years later, at which point Molly began to show anxiety again. Mary decided to try energy healing on her instead of giving her the medication suggested by her veterinarian.

Molly dramatically improved and felt more confident after a few energy healing sessions, but Mary could still detect a consistent, underlying level of fear in her beloved dog. Mary herself had begun a deep inner healing journey the previous year and was more aware of the inner dynamics of the animal-human healing partnership. She would look at sweet Molly and ask, "What are you carrying or reflecting for me?"

Mary recognized and understood the fear that sensitive Molly exhibited because she herself had been born into a wounded family and had experienced abuse as a child. Mary's first serious long-term relationship also turned out to be one in which she'd been emotionally and physically abused. Even though she would eventually break free of the cycle of abuse she still had repressed underlying fears.

Molly and Mary have an emotional wound contract to heal their invasiveness wound. They agreed to come together at exactly this time of Mary's life to lovingly reflect their wounds and allow a deeper level of healing to transpire.

Interestingly, Mary recently shared that she'd signed up to become a chaplain in her spiritual community. From the moment she began the chaplain training program, she had a high level of fear when she tried to find the right words to use with those seeking consolation. She identified that this stemmed primarily from a fear of looking ridiculous, which was rooted in the same childhood fears that had developed as a result of her having been abused. An invasiveness wound can be formed as a result of having been over-controlled, abused, humiliated, or any combination of these.

As part of the chaplain training Mary had to console and say a prayer to a fellow chaplain trainee. She experienced a heightened level of fear and anxiety, worried that she wouldn't find the right words and would appear foolish. She closed her eyes, brought her attention to her heart, and took many deep breaths, trying her best to overcome her fears. Then out of nowhere she allowed Spirit to speak through her in what was an incredibly beautiful experience for them both. She sensed that walking through her fears to conduct this exercise was much more powerful than it appeared. She had exposed an old childhood wound and was healing a deeply rooted fear of being humiliated.

Upon arriving home that evening, she looked at Molly and for

Molly

the first time ever, Mary didn't detect any fear in her companion. She was amazed! Mary recognized that they had both healed at a new level through her own courage to walk through her fears. Mary was elated and thanked Molly for her service. She's now aware that her past wounds paved the way for her to embrace her hard-earned gifts of expressing empathy and compassion toward all beings. One of the many rewards that stems from invasiveness is the ability to help others heal, which is one of Mary's natural gifts.

The description of the five core emotional wounds— abandonment, betrayal, terror, invasiveness, and detachment from the core self—as well as the corresponding symptoms that animals have, which include various ailments and different behaviors, as well as tips to help animals heal are detailed in *Soul Healing with Our Animal Companions*. There are typically two to three emotional wounds that are simultaneously up for active healing in both the animal and their human counterparts.

LEVEL THREE: PROJECTION AGREEMENTS

Psychological projection is a defensive action that humans and animals subconsciously use to release emotions onto another being. Projection occurs when one is consciously or unconsciously reminded of a prior experience that left them with an unhealed emotional wound. Projection Agreements are closely related to Emotional Wound Agreements.

If an animal or person has been abused, traumatized, or hurt in this life or a past life, they might project their anger or fear onto those who fit a similar profile as their past abuser. It is common for an animal to have identifiable fears that are a window into their soul history. Perhaps they are frightened only around children, or men, or women, or a certain species or size of animal.

With projection, a memory gets activated in the psyche. This may unjustly distort that being's response because the wiring in their memory is still charged. Thus, the animal projects the reactivated fears discriminatorily onto the human or animal with a similar likeness or behavior as their past abuser. This pattern will continue until they have released the energy, emotions, and distorted belief created around the original incident.

Humans also project their past fears onto those with behaviors and likenesses replicated from the initial experience. For this agreement level's explanation and purpose I will focus solely on the projection that occurs from humans onto animals. There is frequent use of projection from people onto other people, but that is not applicable with the animal-human Projection Agreements.

Let's say you frequently feel your animal doesn't listen to you. When this happens, if you are miffed or angry, your companion is activating a pattern *for* you to change a distorted belief that you hold about *not* being heard, and feeling as if you don't matter. There is an unconscious distorted belief, "I don't matter," that repetitively shows up in the psyche until the original wound is healed. Like a bad dream your soul will continue to create more scenarios like the initial occurrence until one day you have healed your wound and exclaim: "Enough!" And suddenly you've received the gift of knowing that the opposite of what is occurring is the truth. Then the realization comes through that indeed you *do* matter.

In the heat of a "projection-agreement moment" the animal becomes the parent, sibling, cousin, or boss who dismissed and disrespected you earlier in life. Unknowingly, your reaction is fueled by these past incidents, so you project an exaggerated level of anger or frustration onto the animal. This is a Projection Agreement in action! The animal is hoping you will indeed learn that you *do* matter through acting out what happened to you in the past. Keeping with this example, your animal will begin to listen to you more when you shift your inner thinking to truly reflect that you know you do matter. This is done not through self-righteousness but through self-love. Respect happens inside first.

Rebecca & Devin

Rebecca dearly loves her cat Devin, and they have a deep soul connection. He is a charmer and well loved by her family and guests, who acknowledge that he is a cool cat. He has just one negative habit that disturbs Rebecca. Devin bullies and aggressively engages with Little, one of Rebecca's other cats. Each time Devin torments

Devin

Little, Rebecca's response is twofold. She is angry at Devin and fears for Little's well-being. Little's reaction to the bullying is to retreat and isolate. Rebecca fears that one day when she leaves them home alone and she is unable to intervene, Devin might be even more physically aggressive with Little.

Our emotions are gifts, and animals are masters at helping their people to identify and release the emotions within them that are longing to be released. When I asked Rebecca if she had ever been bullied, she replied that indeed one of her brothers had bullied her throughout her childhood. She added that any time her parents left them alone in the house, she was forced to endure, without protection, horrific bullying by her brother.

Rebecca is *relating* to Little through her desire to protect her beloved companion. In addition she is unconsciously trying to protect the part of herself that was bullied by her brother. She projects onto Devin the energy that stems from her unreleased anger toward her brother. When a Projection Agreement is in place for your growth, the animals in your life willingly enact a behavior to elicit the utmost healing potential for their person. It is part of their soul talk. Devin is not "bad." Instead he is an actor in Rebecca's evolutionary soul play, and their Higher Selves agreed to this situation with the highest and best intentions.

Inappropriate Elimination Projection

By a long shot, the most frequent Projection Agreement that I see in my practice, between an animal and their person, is inappropriate elimination. Nothing can stir up the proverbial pot and push buttons more than having furniture, rugs, and other household items soiled by your animal companion. This is a tough behavioral challenge and can bring up a lot of emotions, mostly anger, in all beings that are living together under the same roof.

When inappropriate elimination occurs through a Projection Agreement, and there is no physical issue, it is likely that one or more of the people in the home have unreleased anger from their past or in another aspect of their life. Maybe they're repressing anger toward a spouse, friend, coworker, or boss. Once the person raises their awareness to see where they are *not expressing* themselves, then their animal will no longer need to mirror it for them in order to draw their attention to the anger.

Many clients I've worked with who have cats that sometimes urinate outside the litter box have noticed that their cat's inappropriate behavior worsens when they themselves are angry with someone in another aspect of their life. Sometimes just the awareness of having unexpressed anger and moving it out in healthy ways, versus directing it on the cat, is all that's needed for the cat to shift its behavior. There are other possibilities, however, apart from a Projection Agreement, which may explain why an animal urinates inappropriately, so it's not always a projection of their repressed human's anger.

Counter-Projection through Your Animal

Animals can also detect their person's projections and mirror them back to their human through energy transference. When I was facilitating a workshop years ago about the mirroring between humans and animals, one attendee had a question that made my hair stand on end. He wanted to know why his dog became aggressive only toward people of color when he took him to the free-roaming dog park. He added that he was baffled by his dog's behavior because he knew of nothing in his animal companion's background that might cause this reaction.

I suggested that he look within to see if there was any unhealed wound in his own past around people of color that his dog was drawing his attention to. The reaction on the man's face implied that I'd hit the mark with my comment. He nodded and said thanks.

After the workshop he approached me and acknowledged what I'd suspected, that he indeed had an unhealed wound in his past that led him to have anger toward people of color. He thanked me for the insight. I reminded him that his dog was the one that deserved the appreciation for mirroring and guiding him in the direction that he needed to go in order to be able to heal.

The energy of Projection Agreements calls in a particular behavior to bring focus to an unhealed wound. Our best two- and four-legged teachers (and soul friends) have agreed to push our buttons to help us heal. There are also positive projections between humans and animals, but these exist at a much higher vibration, which is described in The Pinnacle Teachings level, level seven (see page 102).

LEVEL FOUR: KARMA AGREEMENTS

Gigi & Wilson

My friend Gigi Graves, director of Our Pal's Place (OPP), shared with me the history of a dog named Wilson, a rescue they'd recently brought into their facility. She'd learned that Wilson had quite the story. If you have ever worked in rescue or adopted a rescue animal, you already know that they *all* have a story. And as you might recall from chapter 3, "The Soul History of Animals," every experience has been divinely orchestrated for the growth of the animal and the humans they meet along the way. Wilson's Karma Agreement story is remarkable.

As the story goes, a woman arrived at a gas station one day with Wilson with the hope of finding someone who would give the dog a home. She told the gas station employee that her husband had killed their other three dogs and she wanted to save Wilson before the same thing happened to him. The young man felt he had no choice and decided to take the dog home even though he didn't know how his family would be able to take care of it.

Wilson lived outdoors in a makeshift doghouse in their backyard. Soon thereafter, he met his soul mate, Sky, and well . . . a couple of months later, Sky gave birth to eleven puppies in the garage. Three didn't make it. At this point the family began to realize they were in over their heads and unable to properly care for the dogs. Apparently this was Sky's second litter, and she was only a year old. One of their neighbors wanted to help and got involved. She reached out to several animal rescue organizations, including Our Pal's Place. Subsequently, Gigi and the OPP crew headed to north

Wilson
Photo by Kendra McCool Photography

Georgia to retrieve the canine family of ten and bring them into their facility to help them heal and find forever loving homes.

Unquestionably Wilson has Karma Agreements with many humans who are apparently driven to help him as he navigates through his eventful life. Gigi, in her infinite and conscious rescue wisdom, pointed out how the first lady probably risked a lot to try to save Wilson. And the young man at the gas station took him home knowing that his family wouldn't be able to provide for him. However, he hadn't wanted to see Wilson go back to an environment where he might lose his life. The dog even manifested being relocated to OPP, known for their stellar reputation, integrity, and exemplary treatment of the animals they bring into their system.

At OPP the canine family was very well cared for until their forever persons arrived. I will be anxiously waiting to hear how the rest of Wilson's story unfolds and how many more people's lives he will touch. Wilson appears to be on a journey to something much greater, given that so many acts of kindness have been bestowed upon him. It is as if he is divinely protected.

It's apparent that each person who was motivated to help Wilson—the woman, the young man, the neighbor, and even Gigi—had Karma Agreements with him to balance the energy between them. Upon hearing Wilson's story, it's easy to see his hardships. One might choose to perceive he has been a victim many times over. However, the higher perspective is the awareness that Wilson's soul actively participated in creating and planning his experiences. It helps to recognize that Wilson is not a victim but an active participant in his life, with a multitude of soul agreements. Shifting to a new vantage point allows the awareness of his path to reveal his many blessings.

As I mentioned in the chapter pertaining to soul history, karma is the divine balancer of your conscious and unconscious experiences and the feelings and beliefs birthed from your past choices. Most of the time karma is cleared through an act of kindness that has been prearranged to balance the energy between two beings. This can entail saving its life, caretaking, or as small a deed as being the nice neighbor who helps to connect two parties on behalf of an animal.

Karma weaves a thread through all of our experiences. I think of it as an active strand of energy connecting each being with all those their soul has met and been influenced by on their journey in good ways and not so good ways. The karmic strands of energy are instinctively and constantly pursuing equilibrium in the same way that your body automatically seeks to achieve a state of wellness. Balancing karma from past lives is planned between souls prior to incarnating, and that includes animal souls.

During my cat MaiTai's eighteenth and final year, I treated him as though he were in hospice care. He had several health issues during that time as his body began shutting down. I was adamant about practicing what I teach and staying detached from the outcome of how long he chose to stay, while providing him the tender loving care he needed and deserved until it was his time to transition. I did not fear losing him. Our bond was and still is incredibly strong, and I knew we would forever be connected. Still I always felt it was significant and important that we had those last eighteen months or so when I provided the extra caretaking and tended to his needs. It was as if I was steered and instinctively guided by an arranged soul agreement. I sensed that balancing our karma was an important piece of that period of our time together.

Kindness to all animals benefits your good karma pool. Most humans have had multiple lives of not being kind to animals. Thus, it's important to do what you can to help all animals, which includes both farm animals and animals in nature, to balance your karma.

You have probably set up many Karma Agreements with animals in nature to exhibit kindness to them and perhaps even take action on their behalf. Follow your inner nudges if you feel guided to provide water during droughts or food during inclement weather. If you've ever gone out of your way to help an animal in its natural environment it's very possible that your encounter was done according to an agreement to balance your karma.

Animal lovers have all experienced times that they were compelled to take action to help an animal. Perhaps it was a dog that got out of its fence or you helped to save a kitten or a bird that was injured. To the best of my knowledge there's no such thing as creating too much good karma. So heads-up for these and all potential balancing Karma Agreements you have with every species of animal. Being more conscious of how karma operates allows everyone to take steps in their present life to balance any past karma with animals by serving animals in large and small ways. All animals feel love.

LEVEL FIVE: UNCONSCIOUS MIRROR AGREEMENTS

The Unconscious Mirror Agreements, once identified, are truly fascinating. They arrive with messages from your animal, typically through a behavior they are exhibiting. These messages give you a deeper insight into yourself. Animals are masters at picking up on the repressed emotions of their humans and willingly agree to enact a behavior with the hope that their person will see the message it contains.

The miraculous part is that once the hidden message from

the animal's unconscious mirror comes into your awareness, there can be an immediate positive shift of energy between you and your animal, and the behavior the animal is exhibiting can stop on a dime. Typically, the animal is trying to help you to release emotions around a situation in your life that you're not seeing clearly.

The Unconscious Mirror Agreements are typically more present in your day-to-day life rather than being tied to a deep-seated pattern or wound, though all of the agreements can dance together in perfect synchronicity.

Patty & Gizmo

A workshop attendee by the name of Patty calmly inquired as to why her cat Gizmo consistently urinated on the guest room bed and pillow. Through my questions I discovered that Gizmo was healthy and didn't have any physical issues. He used the litter box and didn't urinate outside of the box anywhere else in the house—only on the guest room bed.

Patty had washed and changed the pillowcase and bedcovers more than once before deciding the only solution was to keep the door to the room shut. She was unfamiliar with the previous owners of the house and any happenings in that particular bedroom. No one, since she'd been living there, had stayed in the room other than guests. And Gizmo had never reacted negatively to having guests stay in the house or in that room.

Right when I thought the reason for Gizmo's behavior would be filed into the "it's a puzzle" category, I had a light bulb moment and asked, "But how do *you* feel about having guests in the house?" Patty's response was instantaneous as she revealed with utmost clarity that she *hated* having guests in the home. She elaborated that there was nothing she enjoyed about having guests stay in the house.

Gizmo was unconsciously mirroring and expressing the

frustration and anxiety that Patty felt when someone was visiting and sleeping in the guest bed. He picked up the energy of her thoughts and expressed the emotions related to them.

Patty disclosed sometime after the workshop that even with the knowledge of the unconscious soul agreement with her much-loved cat, she still didn't trust Gizmo enough to leave the bedroom door open. She didn't want to risk his urinating on the bed again, which is understandable.

She did reveal, however, that a few months prior Gizmo had begun meowing outside the guest room door, suddenly quite fixated on spending time in that bedroom again. Patty began letting him in the room every few days upon his insistence. Each time Gizmo used the time to take a nice long nap on the bed. Not once has he urinated on the bed or the pillows.

At a soul level, these agreements are created to reflect back to the person something they are wanting to heal and/or release. In this situation, it was Patty's frustration and the anxiety she felt when guests were visiting, which is out of alignment with what she truly desires. Patty's soul wants her to find peace and even enjoy having guests or her Higher Self would not have created this scenario with Gizmo. When she finds more peace and joy in the visits from her guests, Gizmo's undesired behavior will be a moot point.

When energy is out of balance, it opens a window of opportunity for your animals to *agree* to show you what's up for healing and yearning to get back in alignment. With these agreements, once the animal's message is received, the animal's behavior will frequently cease.

LEVEL SIX: SYMBOLISM AGREEMENTS

Symbolism embodies the expression *life is like a dream*. The world of symbolism was new to me two decades ago, and I was quickly captivated by its mystical wisdom and was eager to learn more. I actively engaged in study about how to interpret dreams, in addition to the symbolism found in nature and in the animal kingdom, and quickly realized the importance of this amazing life tool. The spirit world frequently communicates in symbols as well, so I became an avid pupil to discover how it functions in all dimensions of life.

A Symbolism Agreement can be likened to having a personalized soul reflector that automatically responds and beautifully choreographs what is transpiring in your inner world and shifts it into the outer world. This phenomenon gifts you a reality check because every circumstance that is happening in your physical world is symbolic of what is happening *within* you.

My dear friend Helen and I are forever seeking the symbolism within each situation because we recognize it acts like a compass for our day-to-day soul journey. The other day Helen's internet went out and the cable company determined the wiring was so old in their house that it needed to be completely rewired and upgraded. While many might interpret the cable going out and being rewired as a negative occurrence, by interpreting the incident's symbolism, we discovered that it represented that Helen's *internal connection* (within herself) was being upgraded and rewired.

Symbolism Agreements with Animals

The animal-human Symbolism Agreements arrive through the behaviors and actions of your animal companions or animals in nature. Sometimes there is symbolism in the qualities of a particular animal species. These sometimes spontaneous agreements are ways that your pets and animals in nature can provide you with assistance in obtaining answers to questions or situations that are "up" for you in any given moment.

Symbolism can also be a divine source of guidance, indicating a need for better self-care and, when necessary, the receiving of much deeper symbolic messages. Like all of the agreement types, animals willingly partake in Symbolism Agreements for your mutual growth.

Most of the time the animal is simply doing what it's wired to automatically do, and in the center of their action or behavior is a symbolic message for you. Maybe you've been very hard on yourself and stressed out, feeling in that moment that the situation is dire. That's where I was emotionally when I looked in my backyard and saw several deer very close to the house. I zeroed in on one deer that had a small fawn it was gently nurturing. The deer was lovingly grooming and nurturing the wee one ever so gently as it leaned into her more for support. In that precise moment I realized why I'd been drawn to the window at that exact moment and spotted the deer. I needed the reminder that my soul's deepest longing was to nurture and be kind to myself, with a special focus on my inner child. Message received, that's exactly what I did, and it was the perfect recipe to generate a "lift and shift."

Typically if there is a Symbolism Agreement in the works seeking your attention, you'll instinctively be drawn to perceive what your animal is doing, or what an animal in nature is doing. The indicator to know if it's a Symbolism Agreement is to determine whether the animal's action or behavior is out of the ordinary, which in turn causes you to detect its presence. If it goes out of its way to draw your attention to it, it is likely there is a message for you.

One day Bodhi was relentlessly, albeit unsuccessfully, attempting to open a kitchen cabinet door that has a child safety lock on it, while I was simultaneously contemplating something in my life that I'd been repeatedly trying to accomplish without success. Coincidence? Not a chance. Bodhi agreed to interact with my thoughts on my behalf so I would see the obvious: that the issue I was contemplating would be unsuccessful if I continued using the same approach hoping for a different outcome.

Once you become aware of the masterful and profound dream world we live in and how symbols reveal themselves, you will start vibrating at a new frequency that allows your animals and nature to gift you with even more answers at just the right time. Notice what you are thinking about when you see something happening in your animal that is getting your attention or what is "up" for you in that moment. That is usually the first clue to understanding the message of the symbolism.

In the following example there is a Symbolism Agreement with more than one animal companion on behalf of its "mom" so she can connect with the bigger picture around a subject in her life to promote positive changes in her inner and outer environment.

Mary Kathleen & Scruffy

Last week I facilitated a Tandem Healing session on an adorable little dog named Scruffy and her two-legged mom, Mary Kathleen. Scruffy had unfortunately been recently bullied and aggressively attacked by another dog that Mary Kathleen rescued and attempted to integrate into her fur family. Upon initially meeting Millie, the new rescue dog, Mary Kathleen was immediately drawn to her, and they made a heart connection. Mary Kathleen was especially sympathetic to Millie's high level of anxiety about being stuck in a run at the rescue organization. She felt a strong internal pull to get Millie out of her discomfort and adopt her.

Being an avid animal lover, Mary Kathleen was hoping that love would heal Millie's fears and spontaneous aggression. She felt Millie was misunderstood. Ultimately, she gave Millie many chances, but after her consistent aggression toward Mary Kathleen's other animals, especially toward Scruffy, she sadly had to make the difficult choice to lovingly return Millie.

Toward the end of Scruffy and Mary Kathleen's Tandem Healing session, I witnessed Scruffy's and Mary Kathleen's Higher Selves in a soul chat room. Their Higher Selves brought into my awareness that they had planned the entire incident for Mary Kathleen's growth for what it symbolically represented in her life. Then I heard the words *tell her that I forgive her.*

Upon sharing what I witnessed in the soul chat room, the emotional truth of the words hit home with Mary Kathleen. She realized that the accuracy of both of the dogs' actions—one feeling bullied, and the other feeling trapped and misunderstood—unerringly

Scruffy

symbolically reflected what she was going through at work. As it turned out, she'd been feeling bullied by her boss and trapped and misunderstood in her job. Mary Kathleen also expressed that she'd been repeatedly asking for Scruffy's forgiveness, and Scruffy gifted Mary Kathleen with precisely what she needed to feel better.

Scruffy was thoroughly examined by Mary Kathleen's veterinarian, who determined that she would be okay. Mary Kathleen is grateful to both dogs for their wisdom and perfect timing in providing her with an important message through their Symbolism Agreement.

Animals That Are Returned/Rehomed

Having to return or rehome an animal is frequently a trigger for many animal lovers and rescuers. Believing that all souls are a spark of the Divine, animal lovers hope that every animal is able to heal from their past emotional and physical wounds and heal in a more loving environment. But it has to be the right environment for all beings involved to be a long-term fit. For instance, perhaps Millie would have had a better chance of healing her emotional wounds if she were the only animal in the house.

In a situation of a pet being returned or rehomed, there are endless possible scenarios that can be part of the animal's higher purpose and evolutionary plan. If the animal has an unhealed emotional wound of abandonment that it wants to heal, it will repeatedly be abandoned until the animal pivots internally, begins to heal the original emotional wound, and realizes that it is lovable. Or perhaps the animal will be adopted by a person who also has an unhealed emotional wound of abandonment wherein their souls have an agreement, with their sights set on healing together.

In the same way as humans, sometimes it's part of the animal's soul plan to have experiences in several relationships and home environments. They can also choose to have soul contracts with many people and animals for their soul's development. If you have returned an animal and are harboring any guilt or self-judgment, know that there was likely a higher purpose and reason for your actions.

If you were motivated to return or rehome an animal, it is probable that the animal had a soul plan to experience another person and home environment. Find and express compassion and kindness to yourself. In situations where the animal and person were only together briefly, it is likely that their soul contracts were completed.

LEVEL SEVEN: THE PINNACLE TEACHINGS

Joy, patience, self-love, grace, acceptance, compassion, unconditional love, trust, and empathy are some of the gifts of the Pinnacle Teachings. Receiving and integrating any of these virtues are game changers for experiencing a better quality of life. These summit level agreements hold the highest vibration of love and light possible.

Humans who have experienced a relationship with an animal that instilled one of these teachings in them will forever hold that animal in the highest esteem. They were eternally changed for the better by the animal, and the relationship undoubtedly transformed the person into an animal lover forever. When a human has integrated one of these powerful virtues, they are eternally grateful and connected to the animal that modeled for them a new way of being.

All of the Pinnacle Teachings are highly revered sacred lessons for both animals and humans. Not surprisingly, unconditional love is one of the most treasured gifts a human or animal can receive, as we will see in the following example.

Tara & Angelica

Most people go through life unwittingly protecting their heart from being broken, which may prevent them from truly knowing the highest level of love possible. Then in walks an animal, aka a "human whisperer," and the protection around their heart evaporates like magic. The animal curls up inside of their heart and transforms them forever. That's exactly what happened to Tara.

Tara's friend found an abandoned six-month-old kitten and immediately thought of Tara and her family because they'd recently gone through a tragic and unexpected loss of their three-month-old puppy. Even though Tara had never shared her home with a cat before, her children vehemently wanted an animal companion. She gave her friend the thumbs-up.

Angelica

From the moment Tara and Angelica looked into each other's eyes, it was clear that the beautiful tabby kitten was there for Tara, to be her first experience of complete unconditional love. Tara lights up when she speaks about her beloved cat. It's unmistakable that she received one of the highest vibrational gifts possible from Angelica. Animal lovers can all recall the first animal that masterfully got through to their heart in ways no other being had been able to do before.

Angelica showered her beloved "mom" Tara with love at every turn and was truly her guardian angel. If Tara was stressed, Angelica's purr would instantly bring her peace. If she was upset or emotional, Angelica would console her like no other being by just being there for her and literally sending her oodles of love. Tara had never experienced anyone or anything loving her at her core like this. She said it was as if Angelica could see inside of her soul.

After Angelica transitioned back to Spirit, Tara was inconsolable for a very long time. But through Angelica's love Tara had received the incomparable gift of knowing how it felt to be loved unconditionally. More than that, Angelica modeled a way of giving love that Tara now emulates by freely expressing her love to others. Their love story is a perfect depiction of an animal-human Pinnacle Teaching Agreement.

Animals Are Transformed by People

It is truly miraculous when humans can learn these teachings through the interactions they share with animals. Alternatively there are many animals that learn these teachings from the love of a human and their expressions of kindness. An animal has no doubt experienced much abuse by the hands of people over the lifetime of their soul, so compassion toward all of life dramatically helps the animal kingdom's recovery.

While humans and animals are frequently working on healing and integrating similar teachings, sometimes the animal's transformation, under a person's love and care, is profound. Animals and their people are both striving to integrate the summit level growth teachings—for when these contracts and teachings are achieved, much karmic and emotional clearing falls away with grace and ease.

Light Team Incarnation

It's possible for one of your spirit guides or soul group friends to incarnate into the body of your animal companion with the goal of showering you with some of the virtues of the Pinnacle Teachings in order to accelerate your soul's advancement. In the grand scheme of things, an animal's life goes by in the blink of an eye, so sometimes they will lovingly volunteer for this type of growth if it is in your highest and best interest to do so. In these cases, you will feel a familiar and exceptional connection to the animal.

Reflecting Your Virtues

There is a form of projection termed *golden light projection,* which often happens in the beginning of romantic relationships but can also occur with guru figures or those you hold in high esteem such as an animal companion. This phenomenon occurs when someone unconsciously projects their "golden shadow" qualities onto another. These shadow qualities are the high vibrational virtues that have been unconsciously suppressed into the shadows. This can transpire when a person harshly judges or dislikes a part of themselves, or maybe they feel unworthy and caught in cycle of self-hate. They believe animals or certain people are divine, but that they do not hold the same qualities within themselves. The golden aspects of the self are usually repressed into the shadows during childhood or a past life due to an occurrence in which the person believed and integrated a distorted belief that they were bad.

Enter the animals, who arrive in your life prepared to hold the golden aspects of yourself and project them back to you until you are ready to own them again as *you*. I see this beautiful exchange of energy as a Pinnacle Teaching. If you look at your animal and see one or more of the Pinnacle Teaching virtues—unconditional love, kindness, compassion, acceptance, or forgiveness, to name a few—know that your animal is hoping you will recognize that you hold these same authentic qualities within yourself. Your master teacher animals have lovingly agreed to hold up a mirror of truth on your behalf so you can learn to give yourself the loving kindness, compassion, and unconditional love you long for and deserve.

SACRED INSIGHTS

You and your animal companions are in a heaven-sent, divine partnership. Each and every sacred soul contract was planned and created for your mutual growth. You've arranged for the level of agreements that your Higher Self deems to be most likely to help your soul's evolution. Each experience with your companions or nature animals has many levels of interpretation.

Your awareness of these agreements can dramatically enhance the way you are in relationship with your animal companions. It allows you to heal your mutual wounds more quickly. As you witness your animal's actions, reach for the higher perspective of their behaviors and issues, as they frequently contain divine messages designed especially for you.

Indeed, your animal teachers are divine collaborators on a pilgrimage of mutual transformation. Animals have eagerly, willingly, and lovingly agreed to team up with you.

This is a wonderful time to pause and send love and gratitude to each animal that has touched your heart. Thank them for the enormity of the gifts they have bestowed upon your soul. They will feel it.

What you meet in another being is the projection of your own level of evolution.

RAM DASS

5

Tandem Healing
Case Studies

CO-CREATORS WITH A PLAN

The Tandem Healing stories in this chapter are great representations of the inner dynamics and many levels of the animal-human relationship. They are tangible examples of the potential soul contracts within each animal partnership and as such help you connect the dots with your own animals to determine your agreements.

Animals and humans gravitate toward each other for a reason; their souls know there's a higher purpose to coming together that is mutually beneficial for their growth. Even though being in a physical body comes with risks and the probability of physical and emotional pain, most beings are drawn to incarnate time and time again for the potential reward of feeling more love, more often.

Animals are tremendous partners and teachers for humans traveling many types of paths. If you are consciously on an inner healing journey and awake to the healing gifts your animal companions provide, you can choose to actively participate in and utilize the transformative power of your animal agreements. Together you can heal more expeditiously than when alone. My wise brother-in-law recently said to me, "I never knew a player that could do it on their own, but a team can make it happen."

Animal lovers, suit up! The inspirational real-life examples in this chapter will shed light on some of the many reasons that consciously teaming up with your animals is beneficial for your mutual growth and transformation.

Gratitude to the Participants

After conducting the Tandem Healing case studies, I set forth to determine which animal-human healing stories to share in this book. That's when the common threads of each of the human participants came into my awareness. The one key commonality in every pairing was that each person had been actively engaged in an inner healing process prior to the case study sessions. I believe this allowed them to be more emotionally available and willing to embark on the deep transformational journey that ensued in their Tandem Healing sessions.

Their familiarity with inner healing translated into each person exhibiting less resistance to change. They were more comfortable diving to the emotional depths of wherever the journey would take them with an open mind and an open heart, and in turn, they were more apt to heal. They stood in the light, they stood in the dark, and they stood everywhere in between for the possibility of reconciling past emotional wounds alongside their animals.

I will forever be grateful to the participants, both two- and four-legged, for their courage and commitment to their individual and mutual soul growth, and their willingness to be vulnerable and share their experiences with the hope of helping others.

THE TANDEM HEALINGS

In the course of identifying that an animal and their human counterpart share similar core emotional wounds, I thought it would be great if there was a chance they could simultaneously heal during the same energy healing session to expeditiously reach the land of well-being. I could envision the potential and hoped for the best. It was a research project I enthusiastically launched to determine if a Tandem Healing session would provide faster therapeutic results for both the animal and person when participating in the same healing session. Nothing gets me more excited than the thought of animals and humans suffering less and loving more.

Often when I facilitate animal healing sessions, I observe them releasing energy and emotions that actually belong to their human, which they've (willingly) absorbed from them. It's common for people and animals to carry energy for each other. If the pairing is particularly close, or in a codependent relationship, their energy fields are even more intertwined. So it made sense that facilitating a Tandem Healing session would provide a golden opportunity to benefit both the animal and the human.

 All beings, and especially those in devoted relationships, are endeavoring to transform and evolve their souls through their experiences.

I went into this project hoping for the best and staying unattached to the outcome as best I could. The feedback from the participants was very positive! I added Tandem Healings to my services for animal lovers to provide an option for them to heal alongside their animals. The Tandem Healing stories beautifully highlight how we carry our challenges through our lives until we have the courage to face them, and often our animals help us do just that.

About the case studies:

- The sessions were conducted remotely so the animal would more easily sink into "surrender mode" with their person in the comfort of their known surroundings. Most of the time the human would lie on their bed, sofa, or another comfy place to become as relaxed as possible. Often they would fall asleep with their animal by their side. I requested that they intentionally promote a peaceful, sacred environment such that the energy could more easily navigate to the areas that aspired to heal. After our initial phone discussion and check-in, we hung up, and then I energetically connected to their hearts and souls until I felt the session was complete. These sessions usually lasted forty-five to fifty minutes. After the completion of the energy healing session, I called the person and we debriefed.

- During the tandem sessions, I sensed and felt an energy cord in the shape of a triangle connecting all three of our hearts. The connection felt very secure and safe. Sacred space is created and held by our light teams.

- The healing energy and attention naturally went to the most prevalent need of either the animal or the human. Sometimes the animal benefited more from the sessions, while at other times the person needed the most healing. Some of the time the person wanted to focus more on physical challenges, but most of the time the intention was to heal emotional wounds and clear the resistance that created behavioral or physical life challenges. It was different in each session and within each pairing.

- At the beginning of each session, I asked the person for an update on their progress or challenges since the prior session and inquired about their physical and emotional health. I also asked the person to state his or her intentions for what they were feeling most guided to work on for themselves and their animal.

- Many animal-human duos saw progress in themselves and their animal through the consistency of the sessions such that they signed up for another four sessions to dive further into healing the original emotional wounds that were being mirrored by their animals. In addition, many people began receiving individual sessions because their animal had shifted a lot of their wounds, and the people felt ready to continue focusing more intimately on what the tandem sessions had brought up for healing. They realized that when they continued to focus on their individual healing, their animals reaped the rewards as much as they themselves did.

I intentionally chose the following seven transformational healing stories because I view them as having the greatest potential to help others. Noted prior to each healing story are the more prevalent soul agreements that the pair has chosen to team up and work through together. It is probable that there are several additional agreements operating within each animal-human duo, but the focus of these Tandem Healing sessions will highlight the healing agreements that revealed themselves most predominantly. My observations and insights into each tandem healing pair are woven throughout this chapter. They are set in italic type and accented by decorative line elements above and below.

Jody & Jet
Grief, Loss, and Abandonment
Contracts: Emotional Wound Agreement,
Projection Agreement

Jody has been a caretaker almost all her life. As a child, her mother needed to tend to her brother more than to her due to his hyperactive behavior and daily tantrums (he was diagnosed as being bipolar at age twenty), so while other children were playing, Jody had the role of the "responsible one," which meant she cooked meals and otherwise helped her parents. At age twenty-two, she married a man who contracted health issues that were debilitating in the fourth year of their marriage. Jody took care of him for the next twenty-two years in addition to being the only source of income in the home.

After they divorced she immediately pivoted and began taking care of her parents, who were now elderly and thus needed her help once more. They lived out of state, and initially she visited them more frequently since she had a roommate who could take care of her dogs. Ultimately Jody moved her parents in with her so she could be more hands-on in their daily care. Her father transitioned three years later, and then it was just Jody and her mother. They moved into a new home a mere six weeks after her dad had passed. Jody didn't have time to adequately grieve the loss and repressed her grief to intentionally focus on her mother, who was mourning and needed her caretaking.

When Jody signed up to participate in a series of Tandem Healing sessions with her dog Jet, her mother had passed three months prior. It was a very traumatic passing that seemed to come out of nowhere in the middle of the night. Her mother's frightening final moments were spent on the bathroom floor. Jody, usually awake at the slightest of noises, had not awakened to her mother's attempts to get her attention until her mother was literally taking her final breaths. Even more surprisingly, Jet had oddly remained in the guest bedroom and did not respond to the commotion at all. This was odd behavior, for prior to that devastating night Jet had wanted to be in the middle of everything and barked at every noise, especially in the middle of the night.

These are signs, at a soul level, that the passing of Jody's mother was designed to be intervention-free.

Two weeks after her mother had passed, Jody was reeling from her shocking and unexpected death, but her circumstances were such that she had no choice but to move out of the house she had shared with her mother. Jody and Jet moved in with a friend, hoping to have time to breathe, heal, and then begin to search for a home. Where they were staying turned out not to be a good fit, especially for Jet. So Jody and Jet moved yet again eight weeks later, into their present home. Up to that point in Jody's adult life, she had always lived with another person.

Jody had PTSD from her mother's traumatic passing, and both Jet and Jody had immense levels of grief and emotional pain. Now that they were in their new home, the emotions that had been repressed due to the busyness of moving two times had nowhere to go but up and out.

Jody, the lifelong caretaker and nurturer was (unconsciously) seeking a purpose, and her focus turned to Jet. It is completely normal after a loss, and in the midst of our grief, to fear that something will suddenly happen to others we deeply love. All of a sudden Jet had a heightened level of separation anxiety. Loving mama Jody had a camera on Jet during the day while she was at work, which she constantly checked on her phone app.

Each time Jody looked at her phone to check on Jet, she was sick to her stomach, watching him exhibit high levels of anxiety. Jet consistently filled each day with howling, anxiously pacing, or staring at the door, waiting for Jody to return; rarely did he sleep. Jody was fixated on how she could alleviate Jet's discomfort. She'd tried a multitude of alternative and mainstream aids and methods to calm him when they weren't together. She also projected onto him her preference for being outdoors and assumed he was miserable being inside all day.

During their Tandem Healing sessions, there was a great deal of anxiety and long-term repressed abandonment fears releasing from them both. Jody's mother's spirit made her presence known during the very first session. She was not only lovingly supporting them as needed, she expressed regret for what Jody had endured the evening of her passing. In addition, Jody had absorbed some of her mother's energy prior to her mother's transition, which can happen when you consciously or unconsciously want to relieve a loved one's pain. This spontaneously occurs when the person believes, on some level, that it is easier to carry their loved one's burdens than to see them in pain. This energy lifted from Jody and returned to her mother.

I recall after my own mother passed, I began having physical symptoms that were new to me, like colitis and headaches. My mother had chronic headaches and colitis. I thought at the time that this was a very strange coincidence. During the ride in the nonemergency ambulance that drove my mother to the hospice center four days before her transition, I had a moment with her that I will never forget. We were looking lovingly into each other's eyes, and all I was thinking in that moment is that I wished I could have taken away her pain. This was the exact minute of the energy transference. Months after she'd passed I realized what had happened. At this point I had to intentionally release the energy and return it to its rightful owner. Immediately upon my strong intention to return the energy, I no longer had "her" physical symptoms.

Most of the time people merely absorb some of the emotional pain of their loved one, be that a person or an animal. My account was rare in that I had absorbed the energy that had created her physical conditions, the headaches and colitis, but there are many others who've had a similar thing happen to them. It is probable that it materialized the way it did for me so that I could become aware of the possibility of energy transference so as to help others identify it and release it.

During her sessions, Jody was more than willing to sink into the throes of her grief and pain to release emotions as they arose through beautiful tears. She became aware that she was projecting her PTSD fears onto Jet and feared he would leave her too. Jet was also grieving and adjusting to being alone during the day, but Jody's fears were inadvertently contributing to his anxiety. Jody also had a "need to be needed" due to her early abandonment issues. All her fears toward Jet were *normal* in this situation. Anyone who has gone through a loss has held onto others they love a little tighter as they grieve and heal. It should be noted that Jody is an extraordinary healer for those she has tended. Her soul willingly signed up for these relationships to clear karma and because of this, she has developed and enhanced her level of service toward all beings.

A noteworthy breakthrough happened during Jody's second session when she released an energetic cord of codependency to her ex-husband. The codependency cord between them was disconnected so they would deservedly feel less angst toward each other. Jody was beginning to peel back the protection and heal a longstanding emotional wound that went back to childhood and past lives. This wound was rooted in an abandonment issue and the need to be needed. After that session, Jody mentioned feeling much more peaceful about her past relationship with her former husband.

During one of the sessions, Jody shared that she saw an amazing visualization as she relaxed deeply into the energy. In the visualization there was a giant quartz crystalline mountain that looked like a cathedral, which emerged from the center of her heart at an exponential rate. It was filled with white and gold light. After the session, she did a web search to find out if the image held any significance and found that it symbolized access to the akashic records. This is another sign that a deep level of healing at her heart level had occurred.

I guided Jody to pull back her energy from worrying about Jet and focus on her own self-care instead, which would help them both. I suggested that she ask for her mom or her angels to be with and support Jet during the day, and to send him love and calming energy each time she thought about him. When she left him in the

Jody and Jet

morning, instead of feeling riddled with guilt and worry, I advised her to empower him by giving him a job (like sniffing out any intruders or cheeky squirrels) and telling him he would be fine. I assured her that Jet was stronger than she thought and that he had everything he needed to feel safe while she was gone.

To focus on another soul right after a significant loss of one's own is, in a way, unconsciously avoiding dealing with one's own pain and grief. Releasing feelings of fear and guilt about not being with your animals will help them settle into a calm and peaceful state when you are not together. If you have an animal that you feel guilty leaving, visualize your animal having all of their needs taken care of, and feeling strong, independent, and secure about being by themselves. Then as much as you can, ditch the guilt, as this inadvertently feeds their behavior.

Jody continued to tell Jet daily that he was strong and would be fine while she was at work, and as a result he found peace being home alone. They created a new daily lunch date ritual that they both enjoyed immensely, and they were much more focused on having fun together. She no longer checked her phone to see if he was filled with nonstop anxiety while she was at work, because both of them felt more peaceful and independent than ever before. Initially Jody thought about getting another animal to *fix things,* but then she realized that they were both stronger than she ever imagined they could be.

Jet and Jody have an incredible heart bond and had agreed to mutually heal the emotional wound of abandonment. Jet also signed up to reflect back to Jody that *she* was the one feeling the anxiety and was afraid of being alone. Their conscious soul journey will continue to help them both grow and transform *together.*

Rick & Sammie

Abandonment and Codependency
Contract: Emotional Wound Agreement

Rick is one of the stewards of a sacred piece of land and lives in the main house on the property. One afternoon he was repairing a fence and noticed a dog in the high grass. At first glance he assumed it was the neighbor's farm dog and called to it. When the dog didn't respond, Rick walked toward him. That's when he realized it wasn't the neighbor's dog after all.

The stray dog had a cautious demeanor, and his tail was tucked between his legs, but he was approachable. Rick, being a huge animal lover, spontaneously offered the dog love and kindness. When the stray stuck around the next day, Rick decided it was time to get some dog food and help him to be reunited with his family. The owners of the land had a strict "no dogs" rule, but he had to do something to help him.

Rick posted flyers at nearby feedstores, and the veterinarian determined he wasn't chipped. In the meantime, Rick decided to help the dog get healthy and learn social etiquette skills with people and animals on the property, to prepare him for his life's next chapter. As the days went on and the nights grew cold, Rick decided to create a heated room for Sammie in the hay barn and to sleep there with him every night *just* to keep him company.

They quickly became inseparable. Sammie slept right up next to Rick, and they went everywhere together. Rick even took him to his day job off the farm. Rick's investment in training Sammie proved fruitful. He had a great disposition with everyone who visited the land. But Sammie's *reason for living* was his savior Rick, and Sammie wanted to be with him 24/7 or he would demonstrate separation anxiety.

A month or so later, Rick overheard one of the landowners introducing Sammie to a worker on the property as "their new dog." She told the gentleman how well behaved Sammie was and how much they enjoyed having him on the farm. It was official. Sammie had formally become part of the farm family and was there to stay.

When Rick expressed interest in signing up for a package of Tandem Healing sessions, he was focused and hopeful of accomplishing one thing—helping Sammie to be less clingy and needy. If Rick got in his truck and tried to leave without his furry friend, Sammie would dangerously chase the truck until Rick had to stop and grab him for his own safety. Rick began to feel locked into constantly having Sammie with him, which simply wasn't possible all of the time.

Even before the first session commenced, Rick began making the connection that being with a needy, codependent dog was ironically similar to his relationship pattern with women. This higher perspective brought Rick to a new level of awareness about himself and how he'd shown up for his past romantic relationships. It is no coincidence that Rick's soul called in a dog that desired a codependent relationship. Suddenly Rick could see the mirroring that Sammie had beautifully provided.

Sammie and Rick have an Emotional Wound Agreement to heal their unhealed abandonment wound.

Rick was born into a family of seven children and was the self-titled black sheep. He never liked school and found reading difficult because he'd been born with ADHD. His mother didn't have the time or the skill set to help him the way he needed. Rick's father traveled a lot, so there wasn't a close relationship there either. Rick decided to leave home at the young age of fifteen. He learned to provide for himself by doing carpentry jobs. The bottom line is that Rick didn't get his needs met as a child, which is the root cause of his abandonment wound in this life.

Until Rick begins to heal this emotional wound and create healthy internal parenting to fill his inner child in ways he was not fulfilled as a child, he will repeatedly get involved in codependent relationships. The good news is that he recognized the pattern and intended to consciously heal the abandonment wound that he and Sammie were harboring. He had another motivation as well; he wanted to manifest a new, healthy romantic relationship from his adult self versus from the wounded child that jumped into relationships that quickly became all-consuming and codependent.

During each healing session, Sammie and Rick consistently allowed in a deep grounding of their energy, and love beautifully flowed into their hearts. Grounding, or having your energy firmly rooted into Mother Earth, is imperative for a more peace-filled earthly experience. Both Rick and Sammie would typically fall asleep soon into the session and frequently continued napping for a while after the session was completed. This is a sign of deep surrender and continued integration of the higher vibrations.

Sammie showed me that at one time he lived with another man who had intentionally abandoned him. The first two sessions Sammie released a lot of emotional pain, heartache, and grief. I felt a cord detach from the previous man, and the heart cord between Sammie and Rick was cleansed and purified. After the sessions, Rick unfailingly would mention feeling a deep sense of peace and calm.

After the second session Rick decided to leave Sammie home one day on his own instead of taking him to work. It went off without a hitch. Sammie didn't chase the truck because he was feeling more independent and secure. In the following weeks Sammie stayed on the farm several days each week. Rick was delighted and no longer worried or even glanced in the mirror to see if Sammie was chasing the truck. There was always someone working or caring for the animals on the land, and everyone enjoyed Sammie's presence and company on those days when Rick left Sammie with them.

Sammie and Rick both made progress in developing healthy internal parenting skills so that they could become more independent and fulfilled versus seeking to be fulfilled by each other. When codependency is healing at its core, there must be a sustainable sense of security and knowing that is birthed within; a knowing that allows the being to take care of their own emotional needs by giving themselves the love they seek externally. Additionally, I was made aware that Sammie had cleared karma and a physical and emotional trauma that had resulted from being kicked by one of the horses, Firefly.

Early on in their series of sessions, Rick realized there was a woman he'd known for a while that he was interested in getting to know better. Taking it slow was his new goal, and developing a friendship first was the internal change and growth needed to break the old pattern of jumping in and losing himself in the relationship.

At one point, Rick became aware that he could feel his old self wanting to push the relationship into something more than friend-

Rick and Sammie

ship before they both were ready. He recognized it for what it was and during his next session took immediate steps to work on respecting himself and the relationship more. His intention for the session was to develop a healthy level of detachment. Old relationship wounds and emotions held at his sacral chakra released during his session. This helped him to make healthier decisions from a new perspective, focused on the long-term goal of developing the type of romantic relationship he had always wanted.

When the emotional wound of abandonment is healed, the person's current and future relationships with animals and people will automatically have a more independent feel to them as they will not be seeking to be filled by the other person or animal. Their connection with others will still be very loving, and the relationship will have a new plan and different soul contracts to continue supporting each other's evolutionary pilgrimage.

Today Sammie and Rick are doing well and enjoying their lives immensely. They will likely be together again in another life because their souls work together well and are so familiar with one another, as if they've done this before. Their heart connection is tethered firmly, and regardless of where their journey is headed this time around, there is a foundation of trust and love to ease their way.

Pam & Bronson

Betrayal and Trust
Contracts: Emotional Wound Agreement,
Unconscious Mirror Agreement

Pam has always been an avid dog lover, with a strong preference and affinity for herding dogs. She has an innate gift of helping animals overcome their fears through a consistency of training and a loving commitment to their growth. Pam formed an especially deep heart connection to a delightful corgi named Niko, who steadfastly was there for her through a slew of trying periods in her life. When he passed, she was inconsolable. Thank goodness her other corgi, Shala, was there for her at this time, but Pam was still heartbroken and needed time to heal and recover from Niko's passing.

About a year later, she was ready to begin her search to find another herding dog companion for herself and Shala. She felt drawn to find an Australian shepherd. Pam even knew what she wanted the dog to look like—she wanted a cross between the coloring of her beloved Niko and dear Shala.

When people are drawn to a specific breed, size, or coloring of an animal, this is their soul remembering the preplanned agreements they have with the animal that they're intended to partner with. Humans and their respective animal collaborators will instinctively be guided to each other.

Pam researched breeders online and stopped searching when she found an out-of-state breeder who had a litter of six Aussies. When Pam looked at the litter of pups online, they were identified by the ranking number of their birth order. Number six, the youngest (runt) of the litter, just happened to have the blend of coloring she was seeking. Serendipitously, Pam is also the youngest of six siblings. This unexpected and clear sign from the universe was all Pam needed to clarify that this was the puppy that was meant for her and Shala.

Bronson was six months old when the courier van delivered him to her home. Pam was astounded once Bronson was let out of his crate for it appeared as if he'd never been socialized at all. He hid in the bathroom for hours before she could touch him. It seemed as if he'd never been inside of a house, nor been walked on a leash before, and he was petrified of the car. None of these things intimidated Pam. She was confident that with love and training, she could help Bronson overcome his fears.

Bronson acclimated to his new environment and revealed his very sweet personality. He began to feel safe in his new home. Shala maintained her alpha disposition, and both dogs got along great. Bronson still had social anxiety and was cautious with people but otherwise adapted to his new home life quite well.

After Bronson had lived with Pam for a couple of years there was still one big thing that Pam hoped energy healing sessions would assist with: Bronson was fiercely overprotective of her. When on the leash, he was aggressive and reactive with other dogs. Once, while they were visiting her sister and all of them were sitting in the backyard, the neighbor's dog rushed his side of the fence and Bronson instantaneously charged the fence, pulling Pam and her chair with him. The incident resulted in an emergency room visit and a broken arm for Pam.

Pam was frustrated and in turn further motivated to take action to socialize him. She decided to enroll him in weekly doggy day care. The wonderful news is that not once has he ever been aggressive toward any dog while he's at doggy day care. When they'd arrive at the day care center Bronson was consistently wary of entering the building, but once inside and integrated he seemed to enjoy being with the other dogs. Bronson's aggression was limited to the times he was with Pam. She feared his aggressive behavior (typical of animals that exhibit reactive and protective characteristics) would escalate to the point that she wouldn't be able to take him out in public.

"The Protector" profile* is rooted in an unhealed wound from lifetimes of having been betrayed. It is a reactive profile wherein the

---

*The Protector profile is further documented in my book, *Soul Healing with Our Animal Companions.*

animal truly believes they need to be proactive in protecting them-selves (and their person) from the "bad" potentially life-threatening people or animals that get near their space. There is an ingrained belief that it is not safe to trust others. Perceived betrayals will con-tinue until the wound is recognized and healed at its core. However, when this profile is only "up" when the animal is with their person, it's a definite sign that there's an active Emotional Wound Agreement between them.

I was pleased to hear that after two Tandem Healing sessions, Pam noticed subtle positive changes in Bronson. While on walks, he would more quickly pivot out of his protective behavior, and overall he appeared calmer.

A significant moment materialized when Pam opened up about her work frustrations. She explained that during her entire thirty-three-year career working with corporations, she'd been betrayed time and time again. Bonuses hadn't gotten paid, and people didn't think she could do her job. Pam could recount each and every betrayal, which further reiterated her firm belief that work would always be a struggle and she'd always be victimized by "bad peo-ple" and treated unfairly. She'd had numerous bosses who consis-tently triggered her into anger that she was unable to express. (This traced back to her childhood.) The repressed anger would surface as a smart-aleck attitude and outbreaks of eczema. She mentioned having been betrayed by her family too.

It was then that Pam, in her infinite wisdom, had an epiphany. As if she had turned on a light, a higher perspective and new level of awareness came through, and she could see the theme of betrayal woven throughout her life. Furthermore, she identified that *she* was the common denominator in each situation. In addition, Pam grasped the realization that she and Bronson held and mirrored an unhealed betrayal wound and had joined forces to heal it. Pam recognized the similarities in their behavior and how they would *both* shy away from people. It was also evident that Bronson had, on Pam's behalf, been expressing her unreleased frustration and anger.

With this new realization, Pam was *all in* and eager to begin shifting a lifelong pattern of believing that people, in general, can't be trusted. Fueled by Pam's strong intention to heal this pattern, their tandem sessions then entered a new realm and level of productive healing. She longed to heal and learn how to speak her truth, and to feel calmer and safer and allow in kinder experiences instead of believing that life would always be a battleground.

Both Bronson and Pam consistently cleared repressed energy (unexpressed emotions) from the throat. At one point, I was shown a past-life wound in which Pam was killed by a knife to the throat because she'd spoken up on behalf of something she believed in.

Pam and Bronson

This past life, in and of itself, was likely at the root of Pam's fear of speaking up for herself.

Past-life emotional wounds that had been created when both she and Bronson were fighting for their lives together in battle were also released, and another past life revealed itself in which Pam had lived a difficult, suppressed life. Additionally, Bronson released a great deal of excess energy at his head and jaws from being "on guard" and ready to attack all the time.

Both were beginning to believe in the possibility that deep inside of themselves they really *were* good. This shift allowed their sessions to deepen even more as they released intense emotional pain and anger, which had originated in their past betrayals. Pam declared that she felt like an entirely different person; one who was very full of hope.

She was also eager to share that, out of the blue, upper management stuck their neck out on her behalf when there was a potential betrayal in motion and completely protected Pam to the point that the other person was reassigned. This was the first time she could ever remember feeling heard, seen, and supported in this way.

Furthermore, Pam was proactive in writing down her intentions and made a list of each of her past betrayals that she then released through sacred ceremony. She consistently used the affirmations with Bronson that I'd suggested. All of her work paid off. Bronson was doing very well and had dramatically improved when around other dogs. On a regular basis, he was confidently marching directly into doggy day care and was heeling on command. Pam was even able to take him to the park and relax on a bench, something that had never previously been an option to consider.

Pam and Bronson have come a long way and are an extraor- dinary example of the shift that can transpire through conscious healing with one's animals. These two brave souls have experienced much betrayal and pain in each of their soul histories, and I'm overjoyed that they are on a transformational journey to feeling more peace and love in their hearts.

While reading through my sessions notes to compile this story, I discovered a sentence in the margin that particularly warmed my heart. I'd written during a conversation I had with Pam, *I feel Pam is beginning to trust me.* Indeed, Pam was opening up and expressing herself more, and I could sense she was feeling safer, as if she knew I had her back. And I do.

Amanda, Chaiya & Samba
Invasiveness, Abandonment, Trauma, and Abuse
Contracts: Physical Agreement,
Emotional Wound Agreement,
Projection Agreement,
Karma Agreement

Amanda and her husband share their home with two rescue dogs, Chaiya and Samba. The two dogs have been together for ten years and enjoy each other's company very much in their elder years. Amanda was excited to learn that her beloved animal companions are on a healing transformational journey alongside her and enthusiastically requested two separate series of tandem sessions, one with each dog. Undoubtedly, she was intuitively guided and knew the importance of both animals being able to receive the healing sessions because, as you will read, their soul agreements and energy are intertwined. There was even divine order in the timing of which dog had their session first. Things unfolded just as they should to provide the deepest healing possible for each of them.

Chaiya

When Chaiya was around three months of age, she was randomly dropped off at a Walmart by a woman on Christmas day. The next stop for this beautiful dog was a local no-kill animal shelter, where she was well tended for a few months until Amanda walked in and immediately felt drawn to adopt her.

Amanda describes Chaiya as having catlike traits and qualities. She's very independent and can be aloof. It takes her a minute or two to warm up to people. Actually, she'd rather just let them know when she wants to be petted. Being outside is her happy place. She absolutely loves playing and lounging in the fenced-in yard and basking in the sun.

In recent years, Chaiya had developed early arthritis, making it difficult for her to use the stairs. She'd been very unbalanced to the point where she was falling over quite a bit. The list of physical manifestations continued. Chaiya had multiple food allergies, fatty tumors, frequent ear infections, and, in the prior year, painful herniated discs in her neck and lower back.

Early into the very first session, I noticed that Amanda seemed very detached from participating in the Tandem Healing. It was as if she purposely wanted all the healing energy to go to Chaiya to help her with her emotional and physical issues. It was soon evident why Amanda wanted the focus to be on Chaiya.

During Chaiya's first year (post-adoption), Amanda was in an emotionally and sexually abusive relationship, and her boyfriend of the time did not like Chaiya at all. He constantly scapegoated her, while simultaneously giving endless love to Samba, who exhibited needier tendencies.

Amanda felt guilty and even responsible for Chaiya's physical issues and assumed that her many ailments were emotionally tied to that one year. She related to and saw in Chaiya the part of her own self that had been abused and emotionally wounded during that time. She sought forgiveness for exposing Chaiya to this man and was still blaming herself for having been in the abusive relationship.

Her boyfriend openly declared that he disliked Chaiya so much that he actually gave Amanda an ultimatum—it was him or the dog.

It was an easy decision for Amanda to make. Anyone who has been in a sexually manipulative and emotionally abusive relationship knows and understands the strength and courage that must be accessed from within to leave. The piece I want to shed light on is that Chaiya, in her soul's infinite wisdom, had a plan and an agreement to be the dog that helped *abused* Amanda transform into *brave* Amanda. I believe their Higher Selves planned the actions that manifested her boyfriend's ultimatum, making it easier for Amanda to see the situation more clearly and then leave the abusive relationship. Chaiya and Amanda have cleared much karma in this lifetime through their loving service to each other.

Each session helped Chaiya get stronger physically and emotionally. She went deeper into the soul work of releasing emotional energy absorbed by others, and also into her ancestral history to heal a long pattern and lineage of heartache and invasiveness. Frequently, I observed the energetic release of negative self-talk mirroring Amanda's behavior toward herself. Chaiya's negative self-talk had adversely affected her solar plexus (stomach area) and was, in part, the cause of her food sensitivities.

The healing energy naturally went to the physical areas of Chaiya's body that held congested energy to provide her more ease in her body. Additionally, feelings of anger, unworthiness, and hopelessness released from her energy field. At the end of Chaiya's series of sessions, her stance looked stronger, and she was no longer falling over. Amanda mentioned that she seemed happier and acted more like a dog. She was absolutely delighted watching Chaiya transform and become much more affectionate after her sessions. Amanda said that it was as if for the first time in Chaiya's life she was finally open and willing to receive love.

Remember, Chaiya and Amanda's *souls* had planned the invasive experience for their inner growth. Chaiya signed up to mirror what was happening to Amanda so she could find the courage to love herself enough to leave the man who was abusing her. Today the presence of Chaiya in Amanda's life reminds Amanda of that period of time. Amanda looks at Chaiya's pain and thinks she caused it, which of course she didn't. As Amanda further realizes that there is nothing to forgive herself for, more energy from that period of time will be released, and both she and Chaiya will feel less pain.

Her beloved and wonderful dog freely chose her physical and emotional experiences as part of her personal evolutionary journey to serve Amanda. And Amanda has lovingly and willingly taken wonderful care of and served Chaiya in return. It should be noted that Amanda has proactively been on a deep inner healing journey for two decades to develop the internal resources to heal her past wounds.

Samba

One day Amanda's mother was outside her home and saw a lost and anxious six-month-old Lab mix running around her neighborhood. She immediately called Amanda, asking for help, who then decided to take the dog home with her and to try to find its guardian. Her boyfriend, whom she lived with at the time, had been stating that he wanted to get a dog, so she thought he might get his "dog fix" for a few days until they found the dog's rightful family.

The young dog was healthy and well groomed and had a sweet personality, so they assumed someone was dearly missing him. He wasn't chipped, and no one in the neighborhood had ever seen him before. After due diligence to find the dog's guardians led nowhere, Amanda decided to keep him. Truth is, she'd fallen in love with Samba and felt as if they'd known each other forever.

Samba demonstrated typical abandonment behavioral traits stemming from not having received enough love early in his life and being literally abandoned by his person. *Not enough syndrome,* as I sometimes term abandonment, showed up for Samba through insatiable needs around food, attention, and play. He was constantly seeking to be fulfilled in ways that he hadn't been early in his life.

For their tandem sessions, Amanda was hoping to help Samba heal his abandonment issues and needy behavior. Additionally, she worried that Samba wasn't getting the attention he typically did due to Chaiya's many physical needs that she and her husband had spent much of their time trying to meet during the prior year. Samba also had fatty tumors and had recently been diagnosed with bladder stones and crystals. Amanda hoped these issues would be healed and released during the energy sessions.

Amanda's energy was different going into the sessions with Samba than it was going into her sessions with Chaiya. They had a closer bond, and she knew their energy was more enmeshed. Her intentions were still relatively selfless in that she wanted to help Samba as much as possible; however, she was very amenable to relaxing into the energy of the session for their mutual healing and release.

I will never forget their first tandem session. Samba showed me a visual from when he was in a car, with one of his siblings, and a man was driving. The man stopped on a corner in a residential area and got the dogs out of the car; then he forced them to run away. The young dogs didn't want to leave him, so the man yelled until they began running off in different directions. Samba tried running back to him. That's when I saw the man grab a rifle from his car and put one foot on the ledge of the driver's seat as he fired a warning shot or two toward Samba to scare him so he would continue running away. In that moment of the session, I felt Samba release a sudden and large amount of grief and sadness that'd been created from that very moment when he realized that he was being abandoned. The traumatic incident had generated a distorted belief of "I am unlovable." I also sensed that the gunshot had likely created a fear of fireworks and thunderstorms in Samba, which Amanda had not previously mentioned.

When I spoke with Amanda after that session, she confirmed that they'd always suspected Samba had been dropped off at one specific intersection. During their walks, when they'd arrive at that intersection, Samba would appear to be frantically and excitedly looking for someone. She also confirmed that he got extremely anxious during fireworks and thunderstorms.

Amanda then shared a surprising and extraordinary healing gift that happened for *her* during the session. While Samba was deeply healing the traumatic incident of being abandoned by his person, Amanda was healing a sacred part of herself, which was destined to reveal itself and release in the exact moment that Samba was being healed.

Chaiya and Samba

Amanda's husband was a kind and loving man, and they had happily been together for eight wonderful years. In all those years, Amanda had not revealed to him anything about her former boyfriend's sexual abuse. During the first session, Amanda was relaxing deeply into the session when her husband unexpectedly arrived home. She instinctively asked him to come sit with her, and then, seemingly out of nowhere, she got very emotional. She began sobbing and telling him about the abuse she'd suffered by her former boyfriend. Her husband held and nurtured her as she released the emotional pain and shame she'd buried and concealed for many years. He revealed that he'd always suspected there was *something* that had transpired, but he wanted to respect her timing to choose when and if to share it with him. Amanda said later that she was shocked at what was coming up for her during their first session. It actually took her a couple of days to realize that she was healing wounds that Samba had witnessed during his first year.

The energy that came through during their Tandem Healing session allowed Amanda and Samba to simultaneously unlock and release their past traumas. As it turned out, that session occurred on New Year's Eve. It was a new year and a new beginning for Amanda. She was thrilled to disclose that Samba had *no* reaction whatsoever to any of the fireworks that evening. Typically he would be shaking and out of his mind with anxiety, but that evening he was calm and peaceful and acted as if it was just another quiet evening.

Amanda and Samba consistently experienced productive healing for the duration of their sessions, and Amanda continued to release repressed anger and self-incriminating guilt patterns of the past. She noticed that she was expressing herself more and had better boundaries. In one of the sessions, I was shown a meaningful visual of Amanda's maternal grandmother, who had passed the prior year. My sense was that Amanda, like Chaiya, was working on healing a long lineage of feminine repression and abuse within her family.

More good news arrived on the Samba front. He no longer had any bladder stones or crystals, and his fatty tumors were shrinking. A new diet, which complemented their healing sessions, was the ticket for Samba to shift physically and release the emotions behind the manifestations.

The timing lined up perfectly during these sessions for Amanda, Chaiya, and Samba and allowed them to engage in a remarkable family healing pilgrimage to courageously release past wounds and allow even more love in the heart of their relationships.

Consider Contacting and/or Supporting

Nationwide: Safe Place for Pets offers locations and options for victims of domestic abuse and their beloved animals that they do not want to leave behind. Visit safeplaceforpets.org

Atlanta, Georgia: Ahimsa House

Ahimsa House (Ahimsa means nonviolence) is a 501(c)(3) non-profit organization dedicated to addressing the links between domestic violence and animal abuse. Anywhere in Georgia and at no charge, Ahimsa House provides safe emergency housing for pets, veterinary care, pet-related safety planning, legal advocacy, a twenty-four-hour crisis line, outreach programs, and other services to help the human and animal victims of domestic violence reach safety together.

Lynn & Sophie

Grief, Loss, Abandonment, and Recovery
Contracts: Emotional Wound Agreement, Karma Agreement

Lynn has always been a huge animal lover, a passion that she nurtured in her beloved husband of thirty-three years. Together they share a thirty-acre farm with a menagerie of animals including birds, horses, cats, and dogs. Lynn has been an active animal advocate and volunteer for decades and sometimes fosters dogs for the local Humane Society.

Sophie came into her life in 2006. Given that their farm was in a rural area, they'd frequently run across dogs that had likely been randomly released by someone who didn't want them anymore. Sophie and her sister Zelda were likely examples of this. Haggard, mangy, and collarless, they were walking down the middle of Lynn and David's country road when Lynn saw them and immediately pulled her car over. Zelda was approachable and had a warm and loving personality, while Sophie was shy and very cautious and wouldn't let Lynn pet her. Lynn was grateful that Sophie instinctively followed her sister to their house. Lynn and her husband already had several dogs and were fostering yet another one, so they thought the best decision was to help these two strays get adopted.

Lynn took the pair to the Humane Society's adoption days with the hope that they'd find a great family who would give them love and care. Zelda's warm and inviting personality quickly attracted a new family. After Zelda's adoption, Sophie, already shy and scared, was miserable without Zelda to ground her. Lynn continued to search for a family for Sophie. After three unsuccessful adoption days and watching Sophie constantly in a heightened state of anxiety, Lynn and her husband proclaimed "enough is enough!" They decided to formally adopt Sophie, and just like that, she had a wonderful new home.

Upon arrival in her new home, she promptly fell madly in love with Wilson, their Lab-Dane rescue mix. Wilson was a few years older than Sophie, and she stayed glued to his side most of the time. Nevertheless, with people and the other dogs, Sophie's personality remained shy and cautious.

Their wonderful farm family life continued for the next nine or ten years. Then unfortunately came the year wherein several of the senior dogs passed within months of each other, including Sophie's beloved Wilson. Soon thereafter, David began having health issues, which led to open heart surgery. Furthermore, they made the very difficult decision to sell their dream farm and move. At that point, there were two dogs in the house: Sophie and David's best bud, their rescue Westie mix, Jameson. Jameson had wiggled his way into a sacred part of David's heart and helped him heal from his surgery.

In October of 2016, Jameson somehow got out of the fenced yard. He'd always shown a talent for escape, and this time it proved fatal. After a frantic search, Lynn found Jameson lifeless on their road. They were both heartbroken, but David was inconsolable and never fully recovered from the loss. Shy Sophie, then eleven years of age, was now officially the only dog in the house. It had never been so quiet. Months later, as a birthday gift of hope for her husband to heal and recover from the loss of Jameson, at her husband's request they adopted a Westie puppy. Sophie was kind to and tolerant of her new brother, Finnbahr, and the family began to heal and recover with the addition of new puppy energy. It was a time of new beginnings.

Ten weeks later, David went into cardiopulmonary crisis and collapsed on the dining room floor. The paramedics were delayed by traffic and upon their arrival were unable to save him. Lynn was devastated, heartbroken, and grief-stricken by the unexpected loss of her life partner and soul mate. The depth of her pain was palpable.

One year later, the veterinarian diagnosed Sophie with a heart murmur and explained that it could lead to the same outcome that had taken the life of Lynn's beloved husband. Lynn, being very aware of the animal-human emotional connection, feared the multiple losses had taken their toll—not only on herself, but on Sophie too. She surmised that it had contributed to her heart condition. After Sophie's diagnosis, Lynn decided it was time for some energetic healing for both of them, and she reached out to me to engage in a series of Tandem Healing sessions.

During the first two sessions, Lynn's husband's spiritual presence and loving support was undeniable. Lynn beautifully released through healthy tears at the beginning of both sessions, and both she and Sophie became energetically grounded and balanced. A gamut of emotions was cleared during the session. They ranged from fear to anger and grief and everything you'd imagine in between. The most notable moment was when I observed a man with a white Westie-type dog sending love and support. I remembered that Lynn currently had a Westie, but she later explained that my vision was of their dog Jameson, who had also passed. At that point, Lynn shared the importance of David's message to her, which was an assurance that he and Jameson had reunited and were supporting them.

Sophie

Significant progress was made during the next two sessions, which were profound. Lynn consciously made the connection between her loss of David and the grief she had repressed when she'd lost her father when she was six. An Emotional Wound Agreement of abandonment was in action for Lynn and Sophie to heal deep-seated past and current life beliefs of feeling unlovable, which had been created when their early needs were not met. They both allowed in love and joy as their energy fields expanded and their boundaries were strengthened. Lynn's fear showed her (through a dreamlike visual) a door to the other side. She was scared that if she walked through the door, however, she wouldn't want to come back. Then she suddenly felt her heart begin to open back up again because she had decided not to walk through the open doorway, but to stay.

Through a soul chat room I observed, a realization was made: Lynn and David had preplanned his early departure for her growth. This new awareness ushered in a wisdom and a knowing—of the gifts her soul had chosen by opting to experience so much loss in such a short period of time.

Beautiful Sophie had always willingly mirrored for Lynn the part of herself that had trust issues and fears about letting people get close to her. She and Lynn have become closer after the loss of Lynn's husband. Information came through during the sessions that they have cleared their Karma Agreements through their loving care of each other.

Sophie has always been petrified to get in the car, which prohibited her from engaging in the travel that Lynn loved so much. Recently that has changed. Sophie appears to be warming up to road travel and is doing very well for being almost thirteen.

During Lynn and Sophie's last session, I saw a visual of Lynn initially rejecting and then embracing a baby that someone was handing her. Once she'd decided to hold the baby, she smiled and felt so much joy as the baby giggled and squirmed with glee. There was a beautiful exchange of love between them. This visual is symbolic of Lynn's embracing and connecting with a new birth occurring within herself.

Lynn expressed that, overall, she is doing much better. She is now excited, anxious, and a little impatient for a new, *yet to be revealed* next chapter of her life to unfold. She is feeling stronger— more peaceful and motivated to actively participate in whatever is next for her, Sophie, and Finnbahr.

Lynn had a vision during their final session as she lay on her bed, relaxing into the healing energy. She began seeing images of everyone—human and animal—that she had ever loved and been loved by in return. She instantaneously was filled with the highest vibration of love and light possible from all of these wonderful beings that she had known. It felt so pure and overwhelmingly powerful, so much so that it manifested beautiful tears of joy as her heart over-flowed with love. Then she whispered to herself, "How can I ever be sad with all this love flowing through me?"

Jen & Lily
Anxiety, Trust, and Spiritual Connection
Contracts: Emotional Wound Agreement,
Pinnacle Teachings

Jen first met Lily in her boss's backyard in July 2014, where Lily was staying with her six puppies after being rescued from the mountains. Originally Jen had her sights set on taking home a puppy. She'd been without a dog for two years, taking some time to grieve the loss of her prior dog and traveling for work. Jen's previous three dogs had lived into their senior years, so she was thinking that a puppy would be a nice change.

On the day that Jen met Lily, she spent time with her puppies but kept feeling an internal pull to return to Lily and get to know her better. She was tentative at first, and it took a little while for her to warm up, but Jen felt a strong connection to her and sensed it was reciprocated. Jen's intuition felt a soul familiarity when she was with Lily and likened it to the ease one feels when reconnecting with an old friend, even after much time has passed.

She was surprised that she was thinking more about Lily than the puppies, so she explored the connection during some additional visits. On her last visit it was clear that Lily was the dog she'd been seeking. Lily's transition into her new home was about as smooth and effortless as it could be. She fit right in, and the bond between Lily and Jen solidified. When Jen looked into Lily's eyes, she saw the familiarity of a being that she had known and loved before.

It wasn't long before Jen introduced Lily to her workplace, an organization that helps those in recovery from mental health challenges and substance use disorder learn that they can heal and move forward to live meaningful, productive lives. Jen was astounded at Lily's ability to be automatically and purposely guided to the person who most needed love and healing. She would calmly sit with the person until they felt better. Jen described it as a sacred and beautiful interaction.

Although Jen was unaware of Lily's exact age or her life experiences prior to the time that their divine partnership began, she could easily see similarities reflected in their personalities and preferences. They were both healers, and I believe their souls signed up this go-around to serve others *together*. It was designed that this would be achieved through their highly sensitive abilities to read and intuit what others need to therapeutically heal. Another shared trait Jen recognized and found interesting was that Lily had social anxiety around dogs but was fine with people. Jen had social anxiety around people but was fine with dogs.

Jen has been on a healing journey and in recovery from mental health challenges and substance use disorder for over ten years. She is very engaged in the rewarding work she does on a daily basis, administering to others with similar issues and supporting them in their recovery. Her work, however, can be very high pressure and contributed to her anxiety, given that she was consistently in the energy fields of those who had been through so much and were actively dealing with their own fears and troubles. Given the awareness that Jen had about the trust and anxiety issues that were reflected to her by Lily, Jen was curious about the Tandem Healing sessions to see if it would help both her and Lily feel less anxious and more connected.

Jen's steadfast intentions for her sessions were that she wanted to become more connected to her Higher Self and the universe so

Jen and Lily

that she could experience more peace, harmony, and balance in her life. She hoped the same for Lily. As well, she harbored the desire that both of them might release their social anxiety and enhance their heart and soul connection for their mutual benefit.

The first session brought a beautiful tearful release for Jen. Lily completely surrendered into the energy session. The healing energy focused on clearing and releasing congested energy located at the neck, throat, jaw, and head. I was aware of an underlying, active stream of fear in Jen's field. It was my sense that it had been there a very long time, so long that it felt normal to Jen. Incredible amounts of repressed sadness and anxiety were released from both of their fields at the heart chakra area. Jen mentioned she felt less anxiety and was somewhat less burdened than before the session. This was progress. She also shared that her incredible bond with Lily was unlike any other she'd felt with any person in her life.

When highly sensitive people or animals begin receiving energy heal-ings, and especially those that have heightened levels of underlying anxiety and fear, it's important to move at a pace they can tolerate. The way I facilitate healing sessions is to be a connected conduit to hold space for Spirit and my clients' Higher Selves to orchestrate their session. Doing this ensures that the healing session is designed by those who requested the session, and what transpires is what they are ready to allow.

In addition, if a person declares that their relationship with their animal represents a bond unlike any other in his or her life, there are likely many types of agreements operating between the pair. Animals can get through to people—especially sensitive, empathic people—in ways humans can't. The animals then will embrace deeper roles as profound guides and healers. When an animal is the safest being in the person's life, it becomes their best Earth School teacher and will mirror and reflect what the person aspires to allow and release. A lot *of animal lovers that get emotionally close to their pets experience this type of relationship.*

⟩⟩⟩⟩⟩⟩⟩⟩⟩⟩⟩⟩⟩⟩⟩⟨⟨⟨⟨

There are likely several Pinnacle Teaching Agreements between the two so they will both know and experience how it feels to be completely accepted and loved. Then they can begin feeling self-acceptance and self-love in ways their souls long for in order to transform and evolve.

After five weekly healing sessions, Jen was beginning to feel that what she had initially desired and intended for the sessions was coming to pass. She shared that she had significantly benefited from the sessions, and that she could feel a connection to the Divine, unlike anything she'd experienced in the past. She felt a profound shift in her consciousness and was suddenly aware of how her thoughts and actions had always been fear based.

During her next session, I saw a visual of Jen lying on the ground, watching an eagle fly overhead. It felt like a very spiritual moment. Simultaneously on Jen's end, she shared that she and Lily had experienced a sacred time wherein they were having a very loving, incredibly deep bonding moment. With each and every session, they both continued to allow in very gentle and loving energy. Then I observed they would get grounded, clear any energy they'd picked up through their healing work, and release deep sadness and emotional pain located at the heart and solar plexus (stomach).

Their social anxiety was not entirely resolved, but Jen said with certainty that their threshold is increasing, and both she and Lily are experiencing more confidence in themselves and in their lives. They are leaning into and embracing their life of service, healing, and much growth as they continue walking the path together. Their unwavering compassion and empathy for others is inspirational and is making a positive difference for those they support through their sacred heart work.

Sara & Sasha

Sensitive Empaths and Acceptance
Contracts: Emotional Wound Agreement,
Projection Agreement, Pinnacle Teachings

Sara was devastated to learn that cat allergies were causing her new asthma and allergy symptoms. She'd always shared her life and homes with cats and was very attached and connected to each feline friend. She liked and enjoyed dogs; however, she highly preferred the company and traits of cats. When she received the allergy testing results, she and her husband had one beloved senior cat, Simon. Sara treated her asthma and allergy symptoms medically so their feline companion could have a wonderful last six months of his life.

After the loss of their beloved cat, the house had never felt emptier. Sara missed the company of a feline friend more than she ever thought she would. Her husband, through his love for his wife and desire to find a solution, researched feline breeds. He found that one particular breed, the Balinese cat, consistently proved to trigger fewer allergic reactions within humans than did other breeds. Previously, Sara had always rescued her cats. Thus she needed to sort through her feelings about possibly taking in a full-bred cat. In the end, her desire for feline companionship allowed her to give herself permission to find peace with the decision of potentially adopting a kitten through a reputable Balinese breeder.

Sara's husband continued his research, this time on particular Balinese cat breeders. He discovered one breeder in particular who appeared respectable and had good references, and they happened to have a litter of kittens. As soon as Sara looked at photos of this litter, she immediately zeroed in on one kitten, a female, and instantaneously knew she was "the one." This concept of having an immediate connection to another soul by looking at a photo baffled Sara at the time. She didn't understand it, but the *knowing* was so strong that she and her husband moved forward to reserve the kitten.

Sasha

*The lure between two souls that have signed up
to be together is undeniable. They will always
energetically feel guided toward one another.*

Another surprise, even for Sara herself, was that as soon as she looked at the photo she knew that the kitten's name was meant to be Sasha.

There was reason to celebrate when Sara had no asthmatic or allergic reactions to Sasha. From the beginning, Sasha fit into the profile that I refer to as "the Sensitive One."* The new kitten's

---

*A profile of the Sensitive One is documented in my book *Soul Healing with Our Animal Companions.*

personality was very quiet, and she was very sensitive. She was an introvert and would frequently retreat to her "safe zone" underneath the bed. This did not deter the soul connection that was very loving and strong between Sasha and Sara, who also just *happened* to be an introvert.

As Sasha grew into an adult, Sara continued to worry about Sasha's sensitivities and was concerned about her not having a good quality of life because she was antisocial. They adopted another kitten, Simba, who fit in perfectly, and the two cats got along great. Simba was much more social and outgoing. However, even with Simba modeling a different behavior, Sasha would consistently disappear much of the time.

During the sessions, Sara was focused on helping now three-year-old Sasha to be more confident and secure so she could actively socialize with the family more often. Sasha had retreated even more since a new two-legged baby sister had arrived in the home. But Sasha wasn't missing a thing that was going on in the house. Her strong nurturing soul was supporting her family, especially Sara, from whatever safe place she escaped to.

Sara wanted more peace in her life and was hopeful the series of sessions would help. She felt overwhelmed with the new baby and was having difficulty finding the peace and calm she longed for, and the time she needed to refuel. She'd been having headaches, backaches, and also anxiety about making decisions.

Sensitive, empathic souls have frequently been overcontrolled in their soul's journey. Being overcontrolled creates more porous energetic boundaries, which in turn means the energy of others is more easily sensed and felt. Sensitive beings are not necessarily shy but tend to need more quiet time to refuel and release what they have absorbed through helping to heal others.

Sara and Sasha are both empaths who are on a healing journey together to heal their mutual emotional invasiveness wounds.

During their tandem sessions, I was shown visuals that Sara had been spanked and overcontrolled as a child, which she later confirmed. As a young adult, because of her past, Sara had chosen to engage in a deep inner healing journey and ultimately went on to become a therapist to help others heal. It is fairly common for sensitive empaths who have experienced invasiveness to choose a life path of helping others to heal.

During their sessions, Sara and Sasha frequently simply fell asleep and relaxed into the release and healing that the session offered them. The healing sessions often centered on clearing energy at the throat, where there were unexpressed feelings. During one session, while helping them to release unexpressed feelings from their throats, it came into my awareness they'd had a past life together in which they'd had to learn to live under the radar to stay safe. This past-life wound was cleared for both of them. These beautiful healer souls had also experienced many lives of being very hard on themselves, based on what they'd undergone, and tended to pivot and blame themselves instead of blaming others. During their sessions, I could feel an intentional shift of energy when their mutual attention was directed to focus on bringing healing to the fact that they are hard on themselves.

Between sessions, Sara began to notice that dear Sasha was increasingly emerging from her safe zone to be around the family more often. She also noticed that her eyes looked clearer, as if the color of her eyes were enhanced. Sara's back felt better, and her thoughts about her parents began to shift. She looked at the positive aspects of her childhood and the gifts that the parenting style of her parents had imparted to her.

∽∽∽∽∽∽∽∽∽∽∽∽∽∽∽

Many times when people perceive an animal's behavior as negative in any way, it is rooted in unconsciously relating to them. The person thinks they know exactly how the animal feels because they have experienced something similar. When you refrain from focusing on their behavior through unconsciously relating to them, they will feel safer to blossom in the worry-free space.

⊃≫⊃≫⊃≫⊂⊂⊂⊂⊂⊂⊂⊂⊂⊂⊂⊂⊂⊂⊂⊂

One of Sara's biggest shifts was her realization that being empathic and sensitive are gifts to be honored, not changed. Sara had a big aha moment when she realized that by accepting Sasha's sensitivities and innate preferences she could now accept those parts of herself that mirrored her feline teacher. Sara could finally give herself permission to take the time needed to clear her energy and refuel. Sara mentioned at the completion of the Tandem Healing sessions that she now understood the deeper reasons animals were drawn to their people, and she could see the Divine in the center of it all.

If you have a sensitive animal that prefers more alone time, respect and honor their choices as best you can. Being social and being an introvert are equally good; each of us is wired differently. Accepting that your animal arrived in this world with personality traits and preferences unique to them gifts you with the ability to accept all aspects of yourself. Your sensitive, empathic animals will reveal their preferred healing timetable if changing their social sensitivities is part of their soul plan.

When we accept ourselves and see our divinely given qualities as gifts, we see others through a new lens of acceptance. Acceptance is one of the Pinnacle Teachings that arrives with an extraordinary feeling of freedom and peace. All beings long to be accepted for who they are. To reap the benefits of this high vibrational virtue, honor and accept all aspects of those you love, including yourself.

6

Aligning with the
Soul Contracts

The various types of soul agreements between you and your animal companion dance together in perfect synchronicity. And what a magnificent and beautiful dance it is! Your soul and your animal's soul are at the center of it all, orchestrating every detail of your loving alliance. Together you've impeccably planned every sacred synchronicity and every experience and interaction that holds potential for transformation and healing. Breathe in the reality that you and your animal companion are an amazing and courageous dynamic duo. When I was conducting the initial "test phase" of my Tandem Healing sessions, the dozens of animal-human pairings that I worked with changed me for the better. I am in awe of their bravery and their desire to delve more deeply into their animal soul agreements.

Raising your awareness of the simple fact that you share soul agreements with your animal in and of itself enhances the way you are in relationship with them. Then you can more easily shift to the higher perspective within each of your experiences to better deal with the challenges that are sure to happen.

It is not necessary that you identify each specific soul contract for them to work their magic in your life. Trust that these contracts are operating at the soul level, and then become a seeker of the higher purpose and mission held within each experience.

THE ELEPHANT IN THE ROOM

Too many times to count, people have told me that they fear if they intentionally embark on a mutual healing journey with their animals and discover their soul contracts, their beloved pet will transition sooner because the agreements will have been completed. I get it. There's not an animal lover on Earth who would ever want to do something that would potentially shorten the time they have with their animal.

Conversely, the odds are pretty high that your soul planned your conscious awakening of the contracts with your animals for a reason. You just *happen* to be reading a book titled *Animal Soul Contracts*. Of course, there is always free will, and there is no evolutionary expiration date. And it is always an option to slide the plan to the back burner.

Here's another way to look at this conundrum. In actuality, both you and your animal want the same thing: to feel more love and to evolve with less suffering. Every agreement is designed for both of you to come into alignment to achieve those things. The sooner you both feel better by engaging in your mutual growth, the sooner your quality of life together will be greatly enhanced. Embracing the attributes of your agreements is an extraordinary way to honor your animal and help them (and yourself) progress on the evolutionary pathway.

The reality is that if you zoom through your inner healing agreements with your animal, that must have been part of the plan . . . *your* plan. It is more than feasible that part of the plan is that you move through the more demanding agreements and then have another decade of feeling much lighter and enjoying each other's company while learning and integrating one or more of the Pinnacle Teaching virtues, such as joy, bliss, or love.

Even the timing of their departure is something your soul is keenly aware of in advance of their arrival in your life, so there's no logical reason to fear their early passing. You can trust that things will unfold as they should and that anything that happens will not be too much for you.

COMING INTO ALIGNMENT

By reading the Tandem Healing stories, you can now recognize the higher perspective and purpose of sharing your life with animals. Clearly it is advantageous to utilize the mirrors within your relationships to expedite your reciprocal healing and transformation. You probably noticed that the most frequent agreement being worked on in the animal-human tandem stories is the Emotional Wound Agreement.

For people who consciously or unconsciously depend on their animals to help them feel better about themselves, abandonment may be the mirrored emotional wound between them. The energy in these pairings that reflect abandonment is very intertwined until each learns to fulfill their own needs. As the Tandem Healing stories have established, each individual wound plays out a bit differently in each pairing due to other components and emotional wounds that are in the mix and unique to each being. Abandonment, trust, and invasiveness are the emotional wounds most often mirrored for people by animals.

Remember, there are always multiple soul agreements simultaneously operating within each animal-human partnership. And as you've also now learned, there are many different ways to interact with your animals through your soul agreements. It can sometimes be challenging, though, to remember—especially in the thick of a difficult human experience—that your animals are always trying to help you through the actions, behaviors, and physical manifestations that manifest in their soul talk.

*Your animals are always in alignment to guide
you to a new level of awareness.*

Here are some tips to help you to come into alignment. Doing this will allow the soul agreements you have with your animal to flow freely within your partnership so that you may both further reap the rewards of your time together.

- Make an intention to come into alignment in order to receive the gifts embedded in every experience with your animal. This is a great way to begin the shift within your relationship to recognize the activated soul contracts in any given moment. Your animals will always show you what's up for you through their actions and behaviors so now you can begin looking at them as mirrors and guides for your growth.
- Interacting with your animals instead of *reacting* to what they are exhibiting requires a shift, which will enable you to observe the situation from a different vantage point. To get into observer mode, pull back your energy and look at what the message of their behavior or issue might represent. It's the difference between going to visit your family for a holiday gathering and getting caught up in your typical reactions, versus tagging along with a friend to visit their family and observing *their* behaviors and interactions. It's always easier to see the issues and triggers when you're observing others interacting instead of being in the emotional center of the situation. Shifting your perspective to

observe what is happening with your animal is a beneficial muscle to build. It's worth the effort to reach the higher purpose of your collaboration, because that's where you'll find the soul-growth gems you seek.

- When you are in the land of ambiguity and trying to achieve clarity with any subject regarding your animal, utilize your established heart connection for guidance about your animal. You'll get a strong feeling that a certain decision is right because you'll feel it through your heart link. Make the most of the beautiful and divine heart bond you have with them by relying on it more often and trusting yourself, and them, to reveal what's best for you both. (This technique of connecting with your animal's spirit can be found on page 43.)

- Trust that when your soul agreements reveal themselves to you is a matter of divine timing. Some people who signed up for my initial Tandem Healing sessions (my early exploration of this modality) were initially focused on only wanting to know what their soul contracts with their animals were. There is a natural inclination for humans to need to figure something out so they will *know* the answer. Perhaps it's interesting or even entertaining to find out what your soul contracts are with your animals. But that is not the magic or the purpose of the contracts. The loving treasures of the contracts are held in the living of them. The agreements reveal themselves when you trust the process and find the courage to look within yourself for answers first, then intentionally engage in the agreements with your animals. The souls of animals and humans have not incarnated together to *figure* things out while they are together. They are bravely here to *feel* them out, through every experience and interaction.

- Self-care matters immensely to you and your animal's physical, emotional, and spiritual well-being. Your pets can feel and absorb how you treat yourself, so being kind and compassionate to yourself is crucial for your mutual health. It's no big secret that when you feel better, your animal feels better. The positive impact of giving yourself love, or the negative impact of criticizing yourself, provide very different results. If you tend to look at what is wrong instead of what is right in yourself and your life, your pets are more prone to manifest physical or behavioral issues (or both). I don't know about you, but that has always motivated me to continue to embrace good self-care because I don't want to be the cause of any of their discomfort. You are human, and life is not perfect, so be gentle with yourself as you embrace a new way of being.

Take time daily to consciously enhance your vibration through seeking and expressing gratitude and being compassionate, along with clearing the inner cobwebs so more love can flow through your heart. Feeling more love within will undoubtedly help your animals in immeasurable ways. Enhancing your self-care practices will aid in your ability to lean into the healing energy available on Earth at this transformative time.

SACRED INSIGHTS

It might be long after your animal has returned to Spirit that you fully comprehend the magnitude of their teachings in your life and how they helped shape who you are today. Trust that if it's important for your growth, the soul agreement teaching will arrive on your doorstep in the right and perfect time.

Much of the time, you will have automatically and organically integrated the invaluable gifts that arrive through sharing your life with these incredible beings that we are blessed to know.

Ultimately, each being is the composer of their brilliantly choreographed life. The relationships you have with animals, both domestic and wild, are undoubtably a big part of your plan. And isn't it wonderful to know that these amazing and divine light beams are your copilots? They have the ability to get through to your heart, often in ways people can't, and this can have an invaluable impact on your life.

Give yourself some love and gratitude for choosing to be here at this important time on our planet, for the opportunity to serve others, grow, heal, and feel more love. Remember that life is eternal, and your preplanned soul mission with a higher purpose will divinely unfold for the highest and best of all. This will bring you the peace you seek as you bravely move forward in creating the life your soul desires. And your sacred soul collaborators, your beloved animal companions, will be supporting and celebrating you every step of the way!

Find Your Inner Room

When I first began writing this book, I had a dream one night that a handful of workers were cleansing and restructuring the interior walls in the upper level of my home. In the midst of their tearing down walls, cleaning them, putting up new sheetrock, and creating new walls, they discovered a room in the very center of my home that I was completely unaware of. I was surprised and elated at this fabulous find!

With curiosity, I eagerly walked into the small room to check it out. It had no windows and no light. The décor was old and dusty, dated and dingy—as if it had not been used for a very long time and as if the space had been purposed as a sitting room. I wondered to myself, *What in the world will I use this room for since it has no windows to let the light in?*

Then suddenly an idea popped into my mind, and I knew with utmost clarity how I was going to utilize the newly exposed space. I turned to the friend I was with and with much excitement announced that it would be cleansed and transformed into my new meditation room. I added that it would be the room where I would connect with my *inner* light, and my light would be so bright that it would fill the room and then the entire house.

When I'd delved deeply into an inner healing journey in my early forties, I would weep with joy when I felt a new level of love that I never knew existed. The incredible new euphoric feeling of love had actually been inside of me all along but had been shrouded by my "stuff." My distorted beliefs and unhealed wounds had created a thick cloak of inner protection that was unknowingly preventing access to the love that resides within my very own divine spark.

Prior to my inner healing journey, I'd had no concept of how deeply one can feel unconditional love. Even if life brings unpleasant feelings and experiences to my door, I can tap into and recall my ability to access the love held in that treasure chest in the center of my being. The knowledge that it is always there provides the peace that allows me to reach, yet again, for the exhilarating and blissful feeling of love to help me through the difficult times.

Feeling the love of your own being is undeniable proof that you are the source of love you've been seeking outside of yourself.

Your soul knows the way to your inner room and will provide the means and guidance for you to rediscover it. Intentionally connecting with your inner soul star might be one of the best tools you have to pivot into a thriving life where there is less struggle. Remember, everything in your outer world is happening *for* you, not *to* you.

The key to taking action and choosing to heal your emotional wounds is to realize that the action of choosing to heal, in and of itself, is a form of self-love. Loving yourself enough to tend to your physical, emotional, and spiritual wellness is quintessential to gracefully navigating this human experience.

It would behoove you to allow your animals to help you raise your level of consciousness by emulating the life skills they have mastered with ease and grace. They set an impeccable example to remind you that you too can source unconditional love from within yourself. In doing so, you will, like them, live in the present moment and accept yourself for who you are, with the skills and challenges unique to your evolutionary journey.

Love yourself through transformative times. You don't have to do it alone. Your connected, conscious, beloved animal companions and light team are with you on the revolutionary conscious path. May you discover *your* inner light-filled room and come to know the source of love for yourself that is like no other. Thank you for all you have done, and are doing, to reveal your light and serve and honor animals by exhibiting kindness for all beings.

> *You must have a room or a certain hour of the day*
> *. . . a place where you can simply experience and*
> *bring forth what you are, and what you might be.*
> *. . . At first you may find nothing's happening.*
> *. . . But if you have a sacred place and use it, take*
> *advantage of it, something will happen.*
>
> JOSEPH CAMPBELL

Acknowledgments

It's been a year since the idea for *Animal Soul Contracts* flowed into my consciousness during a morning meditation. As I began writing the manuscript, I suddenly realized that I'd signed up (at a soul level) *with* my new cat companions Bodhi and Rumi, to create this book. The impetus was to help animal lovers everywhere more peacefully navigate the waters of their relationships with animals through a higher awareness of their soul agreements.

My gratitude begins with Bodhi and Rumi and must include the people who illuminated the path so that we could reconnect with each other. Thank you to Nancy Riley and Lisa Bass, volunteers at Good Mews Animal Foundation, for their superb service, flexibility, and assistance throughout the adoption process. Thanks to Good Mews for saving the feline family. And a plethora of thanks to Bodhi and Rumi's foster mama, Andrea Cartier, who provided steadfast love and healing to their bodies, minds, and spirits.

Rescue volunteers helping out at every level—from setting traps to pulling over on the side of the road to help a stray to cleaning runs and cages—are doing sacred work to help all animals feel safe and loved. These courageous people live the highs and lows that arrive with rescue work and continually find the courage within to help more animals. I send gratitude to each and every person who exhibits such compassion, empathy, and kindness to animals.

Endless thanks to my friend Gigi Graves, director and one of the founders of Our Pal's Place (OPP) in Marietta, Georgia, for her commitment to rescuing and transforming animals; her ability to reach for the higher, more conscious viewpoint in each situation and experience; and for honoring the guidance of her heart. I have learned much from Gigi and the OPP rescue animals in the sixteen years we have partnered. Their teachings flow throughout every facet of my work.

Charlotte DeMarco, volunteer of marketing and public relations at Mostly Mutts Animal Rescue and Adoption, reached out years ago seeking healing assistance for one particular rescue dog at their facility. Through that interaction, much respect and gratitude was birthed for a continued partnership. Charlotte's integrity and positive commitment to help the rescue animals is nothing short of incredible. I thank her and the training team at Mostly Mutts for allowing me to work with and learn from their rescue dogs.

When I think of family, I think of two people—my sister, Shelley Westbay, and her only child, my nephew, Chans Weber. While writing this book it soothed my soul to know that their unwavering support was readily available to lean into, and I send them my heartfelt gratitude for the bond and love we will always share.

Maya Angelou said, "Try to be a rainbow in someone's cloud." Through the writing of this book I learned, yet again, that I'm blessed beyond measure with amazing friends who consistently show up as the most beautiful rainbows I've ever seen. The voice of reason, truth, and brilliance while writing the manuscript was my most trusted advisor and dear friend, Helen Maxey. To say that she had my back is an understatement. Her unswerving belief and faith that I could write a great book inspired me to be my best self. My dear friends Tara Green and Paul Chen gave cherished and loving support, insights, and advice on the manuscript, which proved invaluable. Cynthia Eichenlaub brought her rainbow self to several cloudy days and provided a much needed lift and shift. I thank Nanette Littlestone, Tara Hutto, Diane Glynn, Carolyn Purvis, Bonnie Salamon, Shalan Hill, and Kimberly Cahill for their support, guidance, love, and cheerleading.

The contributors who gave permission to share their stories to help others are courageous and incredible beings, and I thank each of them, both two- and four-legged. Each person chose to embrace the vulnerability of being human and share their experience with the hope that it might lighten someone else's load. Much gratitude to those who participated in the Tandem Healings case studies and allowed themselves to look more deeply into their animal relations to heal *with* their animals.

This is my second time partnering with Inner Traditions/ Bear & Co., and they have been incredible throughout the entire process with both books. I thank them for their commitment to create the best product possible while honoring the integrity of the content. It's a pleasure to work with them, and I feel we are animal-loving partners, both sincerely hoping lives will be enlightened and transformed through reading *Animal Soul Contracts*. To Zohara Hieronimus, who wrote a beautiful foreword, I give my heartfelt thanks for her insightful description of this body of work.

A special thank-you to the beings of light who work with

me and to every animal soul I have loved and whose love I have felt in return. May you know in every fiber of your being how grateful I am to share our evolutionary soul journeys. Your presence in my life opened my heart and provided unparalleled levels of love and joy, for which I am eternally grateful.

To the animal-loving readers, thank you for providing safety and kindness to the animals that greet you on your life path. You are the fuel that inspires and nourishes my soul. May you always feel love in your heart, peace in your soul, and the joy that comes from sharing your life with animals.

Resources

RECOMMENDED BOOKS

Animal Speak and *Animal-Wise* by Ted Andrews
Hands of Light, Light Emerging, and *Core Light Healing* by
    Barbara Ann Brennan
Journey of Souls and *Destiny of Souls* by Michael Newton, Ph.D.
Many Lives, Many Masters by Brian Weiss
Rescuing Ladybugs, The Divinity of Dogs, and *God Stories* by
    Jennifer Skiff
Your Soul's Plan and *Your Soul's Gift* by Robert Schwartz

RECOMMENDED JOURNALS
AND MAGAZINES

The *Conscious Life Journal* seeks to be a bridge to authentic living, a conscious collection of wisdom and support, and a reminder that we are not alone in our journey to becoming our best selves.

Natural Awakenings is Atlanta, Georgia's number one magazine for natural healing and personal evolution.

HOLISTIC HEALING PROGRAMS

Kimberly Cahill offers Spiritual Healing, Energy Healing Supervision, and a two-year Soul's Journey Immersion program in Atlanta, Georgia.

Silvia Hartmann's Energy Healing for Animals certification course teaches students how to perform energy healing on any animal and includes information about how to build a business.

Healing Touch for Animals provides a multilevel curriculum offering courses designed for all animal lovers looking to improve the lives of their animals through hands-on energy therapy.

ORGANIZATIONS THAT ASSIST YOUR ANIMAL COMPANION TRANSITION BACK TO SPIRIT

There are assisted euthanasia and animal hospice care providers nationwide that offer pet loss and grief support services.

Lap of Love nationwide veterinarian care offers in-home geriatric and compassionate euthanasia for animals nationwide. "At Lap of Love, we believe that all pets and their families deserve the most compassionate and supportive end of life experience possible." They also offer a plethora of options to support you when your animal companion passes.

Heron's Crossing, owned by Lauren Cassady, D.V.M., offers in-home pet euthanasia and serves Metro Atlanta.

HELP FOR VICTIMS OF DOMESTIC VIOLENCE (AND THEIR ANIMALS)

Ahimsa House lovingly offers services and assistance to victims of domestic violence *and* their pets in the Atlanta, Georgia, vicinity.

Safe Place for Pets. Search the web with the phrase *Safe Place for Pets* to find a safe place near you. The website safeplaceforpets .org provides contact information for their nationwide locations and options for victims of domestic abuse that will also take in or otherwise help your animal companions.

SPIRITUAL COMMUNITY

Unity North Atlanta Church in Marietta, Georgia, recognizes, demonstrates, and shares the divinity in all beings. Find a Unity church near you!

RESCUE YOUR NEXT ANIMAL COMPANION

There are many fine animal rescue organizations in this country and around the world. Please research each organization you're interested in to determine its track record, what it does with its donations, and how its animals are treated. Securing a referral is recommended. Support the shelters that are in alignment with your values. Consider donating, volunteering, or adopting your next companion(s) from one of the highly recommended organizations listed on the next page. Even if they are not in your immediate locale, many organizations are well equipped to help you connect with the companion you're hoping for.

Angels Among Us, in Atlanta, Georgia

Best Friends Animal Society, based in Kanab, Utah, has many satellite locations nationwide

Furkids, in Atlanta, Georgia

Good Mews, in Marietta, Georgia

Helping Shepherds of Every Color Rescue, in Montgomery, Alabama

Humane Society International (research a local branch)

Mostly Mutts Animal Rescue, in Kennesaw, Georgia

Our Pal's Place, in Marietta, Georgia

Save the Horses, in Cumming, Georgia

About the Author

Photo by Anna Rumiantseva

Tammy Billups is a pioneer on the animal-human sacred soul partnership. She is the creator of animal-human Tandem Healings, a certified interface therapist, and an author. She operates a nationwide holistic healing practice for animals and humans.

Her work identifying and healing the five core emotional wounds of animals is unparalleled. She documented her findings on animal emotional wounds in her first book, *Soul Healing with Our Animal Companions,* and has also created learning modules on the topic for animal lovers, volunteers, and animal care practitioners.

Tammy's work and her discoveries about healing animals' emotional wounds and the soul contracts between animals and their humans were featured at the 2019 and 2020 Animal Wisdom World Summit and the 2020 Animal Communicator and Healer Summit. These are virtual learning experiences led by experts in the field.

In essence her work is about raising awareness of the higher purpose at the heart of every animal-human relationship and exploring its capacity to expedite mutual healing and their shared evolution. Tammy's strongly intuitive, transcending way of working with her clients has been described as "soul dialysis." Her work is characterized by great depth and transformational power. She is known for the compassion that she brings to her work—whether it's a healing session with a person or an animal or an animal-human Tandem Healing session.

For two decades Tammy has been steadfast in her commitment to make the world a better place by helping people and animals embrace healthier, happier lives. She's also created many guided meditation tools to expedite deep emotional healing in people and their animal companions. In addition to donating weekly healing sessions to animal rescue centers, she has also facilitated and produced the Praying Paws Animal Service since 2015 as part of the animal ministry of Unity North spiritual community.

Tammy is the coauthor of the inspirational book *F.A.I.T.H.: Finding Answers in the Heart,* and in 2014 she released the guided meditation CD *Embracing the Divine Within: Meditations for a Loving, Thriving Life.* Her CD *Soul Healing Meditations to Benefit People & Their Animals* was released in 2018.

Also included in Tammy's offerings are various online classes and webinars including two learning series called Healing the Emotional Wounds of Animals and Animal-Human Soul Contracts. For more details regarding all of Tammy's offerings and services, please connect with her by visiting

tammybillups.com.

You may also connect with her at facebook.com/sundancehealing or instagram.com/tammybillupshealer.

Index

BOOKS OF RELATED INTEREST

Soul Healing with Our Animal Companions
The Hidden Keys to a Deeper Animal-Human Connection
by Tammy Billups

Soul Dog
A Journey into the Spiritual Life of Animals
by Elena Mannes
Foreword by Robert Thurman

Animal Messengers
An A–Z Guide to Signs and Omens in the Natural World
by Regula Meyer

Energy Medicine for Animals
The Bioenergetics of Animal Healing
by Diane Budd

**Psychic Communication with Animals
for Health and Healing**
by Laila del Monte

How Animals Talk
And Other Pleasant Studies of Birds and Beasts
by William J. Long
Preface by Marc Bekoff
Foreword by Rupert Sheldrake

Shapeshifting with Our Animal Companions
Connecting with the Spiritual Awareness of All Life
by Dawn Baumann Brunke

Holistic Aromatherapy for Animals
A Comprehensive Guide to the Use of
Essential Oils & Hydrosols with Animals
by Kristen Leigh Bell

INNER TRADITIONS • BEAR & COMPANY
P.O. Box 388 • Rochester, VT 05767
1-800-246-8648 • www.InnerTraditions.com

Or contact your local bookseller